THIS BOOK BELONGS TO

Christmas
ALL THROUGH THE SOUTH

Southern Living®

Christmas
ALL THROUGH THE SOUTH

WITH TANNER LATHAM

Oxmoor House®

CONTENTS

PART ONE   32
JOYFUL ANTICIPATION

Even before the first gift is wrapped comes the official beginning of the season—the fetching
of the tree. What follows is a flurry of decorating and festive gatherings.

PART TWO   120
DELIGHTFUL DESTINATIONS

Southerners have unique ways of celebrating Christmas—from charming parades to dressed-up holiday
getaways. Whether by car, plane, or armchair, the sights and sounds of the season abound.

FOREWORD

BY RICK BRAGG

I was always fascinated by sleighs.

We sang about them in grammar school, with the windows propped open to let in the Southern breeze.

"SLEIGH BELLS RING
ARE YOU LISTENIN'?"

How beautiful that sounded to me when I was a little boy, almost mysterious, otherworldly. But the coal-fired furnace at Roy Webb School had only two speeds, as I recall—hotter 'n heck, and OFF—and winter comes late to the foothills of Alabama, which are more prone to red mud and ice storms than snowdrifts. We would stand by our scarred desks and fan ourselves with Blue Horse notebook paper and sing about sleighs and a winter wonderland that might as well have been on the moon. The only time we saw white powder was when it was our turn to dust the erasers against the back-side of the cafeteria.

How odd it seemed then, to sing about sleigh bells I had never heard, about runners slipping free and easy down the lane—I was not altogether certain what a lane was—and waltzing in a winter wonderland. My people had never waltzed that much, far as I know, but they did a mean buck dance if they had knocked back a stout toddy or two over the Yuletide. But how lovely it is to remember it all now, to remember dreaming inside the idea of a Christmas deliciously cold and perfect as a greeting card.

"IN THE LANE
SNOW IS GLISTENIN'"

I had never actually seen a sleigh outside the pages of the frayed storybooks my mother dug out from under the spring seed catalogs and 2-year-old, 3-inch-thick Sears wish books in the hallway closet—there, or on the black-and-white Philco where we waited for the Christmas specials every December evening like a starved dog standing before a can opener. On a sleigh, I dreamed, I could glide carefree across the ice, and, with the proper number of tiny reindeer, even fly across the world. The idea that, when it snowed, you did not have to cuss the Chevrolet out of the driveway, did not have to hook a chain to the bumper of the slush-bound GMC and drag it out to the blacktop behind a John Deere tractor, was very appealing to me. But the truth is we had not much practical use for them down here, even less than snow tires. The only one I had seen up close was not a real sleigh; even when I was a little boy I knew that. They dragged it behind a tractor or a Ford F-250 during the Christmas parade, and the rest of the year they hid it in a chicken house just off Highway 21. I know this because we snuck in there in July and looked at it, in a kind of awe at first, half expecting to see Santa sacked out there with it, reclining in a lawn chair in a pair of plaid Bermuda shorts. But he was never there, and I noticed that the sleigh was mostly of plywood.

Still, as the years passed, I never quite got over my idyllic notion that I would someday slip down the street in an honest-to-god, horse-drawn contraption, a pretty girl at my side and a blanket over my knees, a blanket I did not have to fling off after about 30 seconds; such a thing gets stifling down here, after a while. I once even asked my mother for a small sled as we walked through the Western Auto, searching for toys she would recommend to Santa Claus as time drew near. A sled, it seemed to me, was smaller, simpler; it was a sleigh for children. She told me it was not practical; it snowed only once a year and usually melted before *As the World Turns* came on and certainly before *General Hospital*. Winter was quick, too. I took her point and moved on to a pellet gun that would shoot through a concrete block. I gave up on ever gliding down a hill, Jack Frost nipping at my nose. The only way I would ever escape the inertia of this snow-less place was on wheels, hissing on the blacktop.

Many years later, I was talking to a sweet lady who had known my father as a little boy. He did not give up so easily. He was about 5, then, she told me, when he came to her and asked if she wanted to watch him sled down a hill. He found himself a cardboard box and a steep hill covered in pine straw, and let his imagination carry him the rest of the way.

I think about a lot of things during a Southern Christmas.

I think about few things better than that.

I hear they get a good bit of snow up near Mentone around Christmas. It's high up there in that corner of Alabama hard against the Georgia line, hard against Tennessee. I hear they get it in the Carolina mountains during the holidays; I hear it's real pretty there at Christmas. But I will not chase the cold northward, as the calendar flips toward the 25th. I have lived in icebound Cambridge, Massachusetts, when the snow freezes into big chunks that the snowplows shove against the buried cars. I have struggled along a Times Square sidewalk on an ice-slick New York Christmas, battered by big shopping bags, slapped silly by single-minded women overburdened with Macy's and God knows what else. How ignoble for a Southern man to be felled by a baby-blue bag from Tiffany's.

No, for the rest of my life, I will go South, go home.

The Southern Christmas is rich in its traditions, its own beauties, its own recipes and notions and, yes, peculiarities. It is why, no matter where we live in this world, we yearn to come home as time draws near.

It is more than a cliché, more than a song. The Southern Christmas is not the one of television advertising. It is a sight better than that.

Father Christmas comes to some soggy parts of Louisiana in a pirogue, or a bateaux. In Texas, they build snowmen from tumbleweeds. On the Gulf Coast, they string Christmas lights on their boats and turn the bays and bayous and Gulf into something glorious in the dark. If you want elegance and history, stroll through the lobby of the Roosevelt Hotel, where the white lights glow gold from the trees and—I am almost positive—a besotted Huey Long wore at least one Santa hat as he prepared to conquer the world. If you want to steal a tree from the right of way, head up toward Cedartown or Rome. They've got some nice pines and cedars up there. I know. The Cajuns will feed you rice dressing, and oyster dressing, and . . . well, they'll feed you everything. In the Delta, people take home tamales for Christmas Eve, maybe the best tamales on this earth. I remember a man named Hicks did some smooth, spicy ones; I ate about 14 of them one holiday night when I was on the road. In Birmingham, I know a family that swears by Milo's burgers, eats them before handing out presents. Once, my mother and I used a bucket of chicken as a space heater to watch the Christmas parade. In the five parishes, between New Orleans and Baton Rouge, they light bonfires on the levee so Father Christmas can find his way. Can you imagine, in the days when the riverbank was dark, what a sight that must have been for the passengers on the big riverboats?

Back on the coast, they tell me oysters around New Year's are lucky. My mother holds to black-eyed peas and fatback and collards or turnip greens, and will not sweep the house on New Year's Day, because, she swears, she will sweep all her good luck out the door. In Atlanta, my old friend Susan Taylor baked black-eyed peas and backbone in the oven till the peas puffed up almost like popcorn and served it with cornbread and potato salad and a great kindness. It—and a whole day of college football—was a reason to live.

In the pages of this book is a recipe, of sorts, for a Southern Christmas, though I am sure you already have the ingredients for your own. I know we do, in the foothills east of Gadsden and west of Rome.

Here in Calhoun County, in the foothills of the Appalachians, it all begins at Thanksgiving, where the kinfolk decide what they will cook, and how much, and whether last year's Christmas dinner was worth a flying flip. My Aunt Jo has made pitiful dressing for 54 years, she claims, but there is no evidence to support that because there has never been a morsel, a trace, left over. I love my Aunt Jo, but she has to let go of that stone.

We will scout for trees that day, but we will not cut one till the week ahead. Law enforcement is every-where the day of Thanksgiving, I guess searching for the backsliders who want to get their drinking in before the shopping season; regardless, it is a bad time to steal a tree. We like to think the Good Lord will turn his wrath from us since we have stolen only from the State of Alabama and sometimes Georgia. There is an artificial tree in the basement, in case we lose our nerve.

We will take our shotguns into the woods and shoot down some mistletoe, and if anyone has a more expedient method of getting that stuff down I will be glad to hear it. The 12-gauge kicks a little more than it used to. I spend the whole of Christmas dragging one arm.

We will make Christmas lists. We will listen attentively to the wishes of our loved ones about what they want and need for Christmas and ignore it completely, unless of course it is socks, or flashlights. We will attend the Christmas parade, which is the one day of the year it is certain to drop below zero, and I will spend the entire time worrying that my mother is cold. When she is, she will say it's time to go, no matter who is marching by. She is 77. It is her prerogative.

We will go to the grocery store, the Food Outlet where my sister-in-law works, and buy all the Christmas necessities. We will not buy chestnuts, though we have a fine fireplace. We will not buy eggnog, though I will drink it at other people's houses, to be nice. We will buy six boxes of chocolate-covered cherries, some crème drops, butter cookies, three or four logs of quality fruit cake—my brother Sam likes it, but then he has always been peculiar—and a Christmas turkey frozen so hard you could hang it from a chain and knock down the Tutwiler Hotel. Southerners are suspicious of poultry and believe there are only two safe varieties: frozen hard as an anvil or a cement block, and overdone. We will procure a pound of China Doll pinto beans, which has always bothered me a little because I have eaten at every Chinese buffet south of the Chesapeake Bay and have not encountered even one pinto bean. My mother will sit in her chair as she watches *The Virginian* and pick out the bad ones. This sometimes runs into *Have Gun—Will Travel*. "It takes longer than you would think," she explains.

People will drop by cakes and cookies and homemade candy because my mother is a national treasure. I have always liked the name of divinity candy but not so much the taste, which reminds me of sugar and chalk, and I bet I am not alone in that. On the eve of Christmas Eve, when everyone is too busy to cook, I will go to Cooter Brown's on Highway 204 and get a slab of ribs, wet, with mild sauce. The hot sauce is too much for me at this age, but it is fine barbecue, I think as good as anything in Memphis. I will wrap presents in the basement that night, with the television on, turned to some fanciful story about winter wonderlands and sleighs. One of my favorites is the musical *Scrooge,* with Albert Finney, who finds his way, as Dickens has written, after the three spirits show him the way. It seems to me the little boy he sends to procure the great Christmas turkey for Bob Cratchit pulls the thing on a sled, but that may just be wishful thinking on my part.

The morning of Christmas Eve I will have a thousand errands to run, in small-town Christmas traffic. I will enjoy them all. I will listen to local radio, and, while I am sure it is my imagination, it seems as if some Dickens-like spell has come over the world. The radio seems not so much filled with politics and meanness but with simple music, with old songs about a Christmas that might not exist at all, down here, but nonetheless is part of our memories and our past. I drive and drive, sometimes long after my errands are complete—I see some fine cedars there, for next year—drive until I find that song about sleigh bells.

"WHAT A BEAUTIFUL SIGHT WE'RE HAPPY TONIGHT"

The weatherman, after telling the children his radar has detected a sleigh and reindeer, will reluctantly inform the viewing public that, alas, there is no snow, no White Christmas, and I will think, well, who needs it. Everything else is perfect, timeless. My people will gather on the morrow, as many as time on this earth allows. They will talk of things important, of work and children, and dogs, and the power bill, and some football, and then there will be a grace of dignity and kindness, and then we will eat the food of my people, our people.

Merry Christmas to you, across this South.

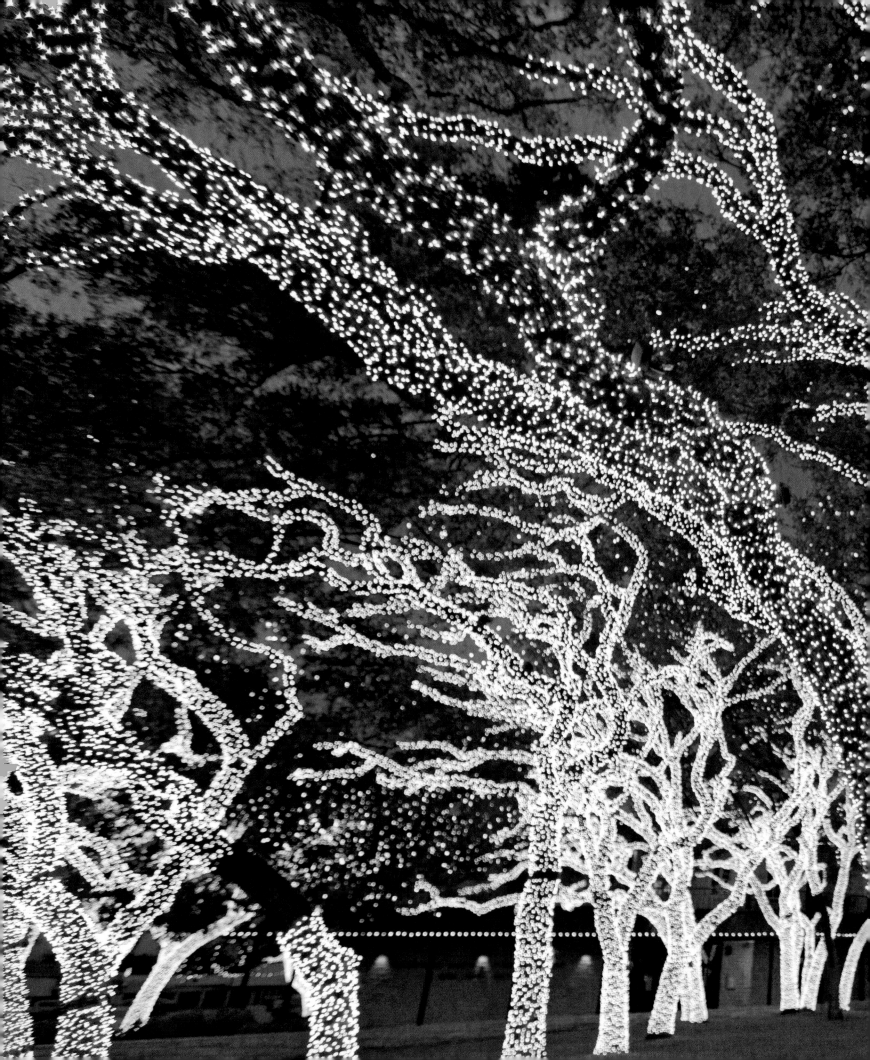

INTRODUCTION

BY KIM CROSS

"Take 40 eggs and divide the whites from the yolks and beat them to a froth. Then work 4 pounds of butter to a cream and put the whites of eggs to it a Spoon full at a time till it is well work'd. Then put 4 pounds of sugar finely powdered to it in the same manner then put in the Yolks of eggs and 5 pounds of flour and 5 pounds of fruit. 2 hours will bake it. Add to it half an ounce of mace and nutmeg half a pint of wine and some fresh brandy."

—MARTHA WASHINGTON'S GREAT CAKE RECIPE

I t should be no surprise that our first First Lady had a recipe for a big white cake. Like most great heirloom recipes, it is a production (40 eggs!), unedited (what *kind* of fruit?), imprecise (exactly *how much* brandy constitutes *some*?), and shows blatant disregard for such modern conceits as dietary cholesterol (*See:* 4 pounds of butter) and moderation (*Ditto:* 4 pounds of sugar). And that's not even taking into account her frosting, which calls for 3 more pounds of sugar and *two solid hours* of whipping.

Mrs. Washington, we salute you. If ever there is a time of the year that warrants unbridled exuberance and profligate indulgence, it is Christmas.

There are plenty of occasions that bring us together for food and festivities throughout the year—weddings, reunions, Easter, Thanksgiving, and the Fourth of July. But Christmas exists in a league of its own. It is a holiday as old as time itself, a tradition steeped in faith, battered with love, and deep-fried in pure joy. It is everything good about life on earth distilled into one season.

Christmas is a production wherever you live. It is why we have year-round Christmas stores that have been in business for decades. Why we start planning holiday menus before the last kernel of Halloween candy corn has been eaten. It is the reason Louisianans build bonfires bigger than houses, and Texans make mountains of Christmas tamales.

Because here in the South, we, like Mrs. Washington, embrace unbridled exuberance. We take our mirth seriously. If Christmas wasn't religion, we'd probably make it a sport.

You may not be surprised that at *Southern Living*, Christmas starts in July. Even as the mercury pushes into the nineties, the halls fill with the scent of Fraser fir. Plates heaped with Christmas cookies and holiday stuffing appear, like magic, beside a certain editorial coffeepot; those who work outside the Test Kitchen know to wander by it at a certain hour, right after the daily tasting. In the middle of swimsuit season, cookie week is a serious occupational hazard.

Meanwhile, in the photo studio, an entourage of prop stylists, food stylists, editors, interns, and photographers are fussing over a big white cake. She has emerged like a beauty queen in the pageant of cakes that parades through months of recipe testing, vying for the December cover—the magazine's equivalent of a swimsuit issue.

Writers are cranking on the A/C full blast, sipping cocoa, and playing "Blue Christmas," trying to trick their minds into believing it is not hot enough to cook an egg on a dashboard. An intern somewhere is organizing cake stands.

And somewhere outside, in some charming neighborhood, in the 98 percent humidity that congeals the summer air to the consistency of ambrosia, another team of stylists is decking the halls—and the banisters, porch railings, mantels, and windows—with lavish winter greenery. A photographer, mopping her brow, is capturing the perfect holiday home, before it wilts in the heat.

Editorial calendar aside, it is no wonder we need a few months' head start to prepare for the Super Bowl of holidays.

The South may not be the only region that goes overboard for the holidays, but we like to believe we do it with inimitable style. No matter where you live, your holidays could not possibly be mistaken for happening anywhere but the South.

Part of the charm lies not only in what we have, but also in what we do not have, and the charm of our improvisation.

When you live on a catfish pond in the woods of rural Alabama, a white Christmas is not a dream you bother with, unless it involves Bing Crosby and a VCR. The best you can hope for is the once-every-five-years dusting of flakes that must be shoveled feverishly with a spatula. It is usually enough for one sad snowball, stained with red clay, that is nonetheless so rare and special that it will be stashed in the freezer for months. It might stay in there forever, if no one ever mistook it for a freezer-burned meatball and threw it out.

When you live in Florida, you make sand angels at the beach and build a sandman with mother-of-pearl eyes and a crooked driftwood smile. You string your Boston Whaler with Christmas lights and motor under the bridge to join the boat parade, watching your own bright reflection winking back from the inky water. You leap off the dock on Christmas Day for a swim around the No Wake Zone sign in water that would make a polar bear sweat. By noon, you're drinking iced tea.

You may live in the Lowcountry, where palmettos count as evergreens and oysters are an integral part of the dressing. Or in tamale-loving Texas, where a year's worth of disagreements can be aired and solved over the patting of meat into masa wrapped in yellow corn husks like presents.

Or you may live farther north, where the snow sticks to the holly like buttercream frosting and the snowmen do not begin to slouch under the winter sun.

Whether it is Spanish moss or mountain laurel waving outside your window, you know that your Southern Christmas could not happen anywhere but home.

Which is not to say that Christmas must always stay home. Some of the most beautiful cities on American soil are even more spectacular this time of year. It is one thing to walk the squares of Savannah in the heat of summer. It is another to see them lit up in the dark of a winter night. They are less crowded, less hot, and often, more soulful.

Historic Charleston transforms like a beautiful woman dressed up for the party of the year. During the Grand Illumination of Colonial Williamsburg, candles wink from the windows like knowing eyes, lit in memory of those who could not be home for the holidays. New Orleans enjoys what may be the best weather it sees all year, and in the lobbies of her grand hotels and the gas-lit streets of the old French Quarter, the city's old soul smiles.

Some of the most memorable Christmases are those that break from tradition, if only for just a year. While there is comfort in repetition, there is awakening in change. When tradition starts to feel like obligation, it is time to set those habits aside for a year and go out and explore. Our region remains one of the most culturally authentic places in America. You will not lack good options.

Create a holiday bucket list: Take a sleigh ride through the snow in western Maryland. Sing along with the Holy Ghost Catholic Church gospel choir in Opelousas, Louisiana. See the lights of The Plaza in Kansas City, where the fountains may freeze into beautiful ice sculptures. Enter the gingerbread contest at The Grove Park Inn in Asheville, North Carolina. Take a boat ride through the lights of the Riverwalk in San Antonio, Texas. See the lighting of our nation's Christmas tree in Washington, D.C. Rent a cabin in the Smokies and have a pancake breakfast in Gatlinburg, Tennessee. Spend Christmas at the beach in Florida.

We promise Santa will find you.

And next year, those traditions that seemed like chores will feel exciting all over again.

As a spool of ribbon unrolls, faster and faster as it nears the end, so does the Christmas season. Capturing those fleeting moments of revelry was our goal for this book, a story that carries you through the season like a river. It is impossible, of course, to bottle Christmas, or catch it between the pages of a book. But we did our best to capture the most universally beloved moments both in photographs and words.

It starts with the fetching of the tree, the universal centerpiece of our holidays. It spreads out from there,

to the swag on the mantel, the wreaths on the doors, the trimmings with which we embellish our homes. It flows through the parties, flavors, feasts—and the quiet moments of spiritual reflection—that we look forward to every year. It offers menus for every kind of gathering under the mistletoe, from a casual cocktail supper to a seashore soiree. It ends with a Lowcountry oyster roast to bring good luck in the New Year.

This book is meant to be looked at, read, flipped through, bookmarked, and shared. It is meant to evoke memories of Christmases past and give you inspiration as you plan this year's festivities. In these pages you will find stories and recipes, essays and menus, and thousands of ideas. We hope that you lean forward in your chair at times, propelled by something you find in these pages. In other moments, we hope you forget the hour as you lose yourself in the words and images.

We asked some of our favorite Southern writers to muse about their holidays, and their essays will make you smile and nod. We encourage you to tell your own stories and maybe even write them down. They are as much a part of a family's legacy as heirloom recipes and Meemaw's china.

While you may find some of the themes we touch upon comfortably familiar, we also wanted to share the kaleidoscope of traditions that makes the South unique. From the opulent Réveillon dinners of New Orleans to the parade of the foxhounds through Middleburg, Virginia, we hope we inspire you to discover a whole new side of Christmas.

Because Christmas is all about inspiration—to love and to honor, to give and forgive. And most of all, to Believe.

We know that Christmas is not just a day. It is a journey, a season, a state of mind.

It is why calories from the frosting spoon do not count.

It is why you can never have too many cake stands.

It is why whoever stole baby Jesus from the Methodists' Nativity that year were ultimately forgiven—though they must suffer the retelling of it every year.

It is why a volunteer firefighter from rural Alabama saves his pennies all year to buy a custom white beard and spends his vacation at Santa School; when he walks through Children's Hospital, the little faces that brighten along his path make him wish he wore a white beard all year.

Each family has its own recipes, stories, traditions, and flavors, as different as snowflakes. No matter what you believe or how you celebrate, these things are part of our holiday DNA, the secret recipe that makes us who we are.

They say you never own a Christmas cactus; you just take care of it for the next generation. We think traditions are like that, too. They have a way of bridging gaps, of linking past and future.

As do cakes.

Mrs. Washington knew our secret: The big white cake is more than just dessert. It is one of the great unifying forces that binds us across the great divides of politics, regional barbecue, and SEC football. It is a work of art and a labor of love, a gift to be shared during the time of year that draws us together no matter what.

And nothing is sweeter than that.

JOYFUL
ANTICIPATION

One of the most beautiful aspects of Christmas is that every year we get the chance to do it all over again. One by one, our traditions—particularly those happening right in our home—stir our memories. They are rituals rendered rote so long ago we can't remember what existed before them. They whirl us into the spirit of the season.

It could be first hearing and feeling the underfoot crunch of the gravel lot where we move from fir to fir until we've selected the perfect Christmas tree—not too short, not too tall—to bring back home. It could be that first walk through a wooded forest or from stall to stall at the farmers' market to forage the greenery that we'll weave for our doors and spread on our tabletops. It could be that first weekend morning in early December when, while cradling a steaming cup of coffee, we orchestrate on our porches or in our dens or in open corners of our kitchens the poetic arrangement of the season's most stunning flowers and plants, thus creating glorious floral quilts bursting with whites and reds and greens.

Sometimes just the smallest gestures send us into seasonal bliss. Tacking the year's first holiday card to the refrigerator. Baking the first big cake or batch of spiced goodies with cinnamon or nutmeg or cloves. Hearing the first Christmas standard crooned over the radio.

Christmas is a tradition that's as old as our country itself, and it began in the South. Virginia's colonial settlers were among the first to celebrate it on American soil. Jamestown's tables groaned under the feast: fresh oysters, mince pies, wild fowl, and rivers of toddies and cider. This was a season of parties and fox hunts, of festive balls with dancing that went on until the fiddler's arm wore out. Christmas Day began with gunshots fired into the sky, carried on with gift giving and bountiful food, and was, as Thomas Jefferson wrote, "a day of greatest mirth and jollity."

Southerners claimed Christmas as not only a birth-right but a legal right: Alabama was the first state to declare Christmas a legal holiday in 1836. Louisiana and Arkansas quickly followed. The rest of the nation didn't get around to it until 1870, when President Ulysses S. Grant declared it a federal holiday.

THE GREENBRIER
AT WHITE SULPHUR SPRINGS

A white Christmas at this West Virginia hotel can be more
than a dream. Inside, the 60-foot Christmas tree that greets
you on arrival suggests the scale of the resort's opulence.
More than 40 trees illuminate the labyrinthine corridors from
Thanksgiving through early January.

Maybe they saw how much fun we were having down here and realized what they were missing.

When it comes to Christmas, Southerners are not known for restraint. Some of us are more zealous than others, but every one of us knows that friend or relative who starts planning next year's Christmas sometime around January, who shops for ornaments on sale at the beach, and who is often caught absent mindedly humming a carol out of season if not out of tune. And we all know the house that nearly short-circuits the neighborhood and draws drive-by gawkers like a bug zapper in July. In their defense, we know of no etiquette law that sets limits on lights or mandates that holiday decor shalt not be purchased until thy first frost.

The timely removal of Christmas lights from one's porch, however, is another matter. We're not pointing fingers. You know who you are. Life gets busy, we know. But for Pete's sake, can you get around to it by Easter?

The truth is that our mothers and fathers and their mothers and fathers and further back inherited traditions and added their own personal touches before passing them down all the way to us. The moments we experience and traditions we preserve at Christmas are layered and woven with generations of details.

At the first hint of Christmas, we take our places as lucky shepherds, delighted to share and guide our family traditions through yet another year, sparked with joy at the chance we have to do it all over again.

A SPECTACLE OF LIGHTS

Dusk is the perfect time to arrive at Noël Acadian au Village, a quaint replica of a 19th-century Cajun hamlet just south of Lafayette, Louisiana. Each evening in December, more than a half-million lights illuminate the village.

Johnson City, Texas

Kansas City, Missouri

Noël Acadian au Village
near Lafayette, Louisiana

Do we ever get beyond the images of childhood? The way we first hear language, for instance (old woman on a porch, talking on and on as it gets dark)... Or Christmas: my Aunt Bess' quivery soprano on "O Holy Night" in the chilly stone church ... the sharp strange smell of grapefruit, shipped from Florida in a wooden crate ... the guns of Christmas morning, echoing around and around the ring of frosty mountains ... how the air smells right before it snows, and how the sky looks, like the underside of a quilt ... oranges studded with cloves, in a bowl on the coffee table ... my daddy in his dime store wearing a bow tie. All my images of this holiday season cluster around the dime store, the Methodist Church, and my mama's Christmas kitchen, always full of people and food.

—LEE SMITH, "Christmas Memories"

IT BEGINS WITH THE TREE

Before the first cookie has been pulled from the oven, before the licking of the frosting bowl or the squeal of scissors down a curl of ribbon comes the official beginning—the fetching of the tree—and the smell that unfurls from each bough. It is less obvious than eggnog, quieter than caroling, more subtle than garlands and strands of white lights.

FETCHING THE TREE

The source of the tree, the size, and the variety matters less than the act of bringing it home. The details vary from family to family, but the effort is always communal, memorable, and comfortably familiar. It is the ritual that, year after year, launches the season of togetherness. It is not something you do alone.

Some families make a trip to the Christmas tree farm to walk among stands of fragrant branches nodding in the winter wind. Others walk into the woods with an axe or a saw. The arc of the hatchet, the sound of steel teeth gnawing wood, is a beautiful sound that echoes through generations. The hauling of this precious timber is a drunken waltz or an awkward team effort, branches in faces and limbs upon limbs. When it is done, we wrap frozen hands around a mug of hot cider, or rub them in front of the dashboard vents, until the sting of the cold melts away.

The tree may come from a Boy Scout troop, their young cheeks lit by a sap-scented barrel fire in the parking lot of the church on the hill. The Scouts pull out each tree and shake it loose for us to admire, compare, and imagine in our home. The choice may be a democratic vote, or the propriety of the littlest one with the strongest faith in Santa. We tie our prize atop the minivan, or lay it down in the back of a pickup, and wrestle it into the living room, raining a trail of green needles.

A Christmas tree doesn't have to be watered to be real. It may be carried down from the attic in a box, its forever-green branches snapped into place and fluffed with no less love and devotion. The assembled tree has its own distinct smell, the scent of Christmases past. It may be of attic dust or a wintergreen-scented candle.

The search for the perfect tree involves fastidious investigation and great deliberation because this living thing becomes the centerpiece of our holidays, the focal point of our home. The Christmas tree is a beautiful, centuries-old tradition brought to us by German immigrants, but we have taken creative license and made it our own.

We grow forests of them, too. Virginia pines thrive from Florida to East Texas, and the market for fresh trees has revived small farms in towns hit hard by the decline of cotton and tobacco. And our trees are beauties. North Carolina, known for its Fraser firs, has grown more White House Christmas trees than any other state.

MIDDLEBURG CHRISTMAS TREE FARM, LOUDON COUNTY, VIRGINIA

Once Thanksgiving has passed, we welcome the official start of the merriest time of the year. For many of us that starts with the selection of the perfect Christmas tree. Cutting a fresh tree offers more than just the spicy scent of evergreen—it can be the beginning of a generations-long family tradition.

"'We're almost there, can you smell it, Buddy?' she says, as though we were approaching an ocean.
And indeed it is a kind of ocean. Scented areas of holiday trees, prickly-leafed holly. Red berries shiny
as Chinese bells: black crows swoop upon them screaming. Having stuffed our burlap sacks
with enough greenery and crimson to garland a dozen windows, we set about choosing a tree.
'It should be,' muses my friend, 'twice as tall as a boy. So a boy can't steal the star.'"

—TRUMAN CAPOTE, "A Christmas Memory"

THE PERFECT YULETIDE EVERGREEN

MORGAN MURPHY

Scene: a Christmas tree lot in Alabama. Time: the day after Thanksgiving. A little frost is underfoot, and a nervous Boy Scout with a slightly rumpled kerchief has been following me around for the past half hour as I examine every evergreen on the lot. Not for amateurs, this business of picking the perfect Christmas tree.

A real tree just makes Christmas—pine in the air, sap on the furniture, needles in the carpet, the whole bit. You can't fake that. No petroleum-based, mold-formed, insert-figure-A-into-stalk-B imitation can take the place of a real tree. That pine-scented spray you've got isn't fooling anybody. Your house smells like a cab.

Let's begin with the size of the tree. Don't give me some sad shrub, some Charlie Brown Christmas weed, barely able to hold up the 4-pound dough ornament Aunt Helen baked and shellacked in 1978. No, give me a towering Fraser or Douglas fir or Scotch pine. "I want big, son, big," I tell the cadet. Every year I buy a tree that far exceeds the house. What caused that gouge down the center of the living room ceiling? The 15-footer of 1998. Those scratches on the side of the front door? That was one fat Fraser. The water stains on the hardwood floors? I don't want to talk about it.

A big tree sports limbs capable of holding upwards of 300 ornaments. Those ornaments can't fall; they're sentimental. If the house starts to burn down, I'm grabbing the 20 boxes of glitter-covered eggs, needlepoint wreaths, and papier-mâché blobs and jumping from the attic. Mine is no decorator tree, headed for the cover of a magazine. It isn't flocked. It doesn't have coordinated lavender balls and ribbon. My memories don't match furniture.

The tree has to be fresh because there's no way I'm stringing those tiny modern lights that blink to "Jingle Bells." My lights were stolen off the runway at LaGuardia. Our electrician had to wire a dedicated "tree circuit." The power company sends me a fruitcake every year. Think of those big C9 "fire-starter" bulbs from the 1950s, and you'll get the idea. Carolers at my house wear SPF 30.

Maybe this whole tree obsession comes from the time my parents returned home to find me and the 90-year-old babysitter trapped under their fallen tannenbaum. Or from my first Christmas with spectacles: Mama taught me to take off my glasses and look at the lights. (You perfect-vision types have no idea what you're missing.)

I remember many Christmases and many trees. Some years we sang around them; some we sat under them, opening gifts after relatives left. Other years, I stared at the tree in the dark, pondering the majesty of a 2,000-year-old miracle. Those memories, contrary to what people might say, are the kind that can be placed carefully in a box and brought out to hang on next year's tree. They're what really make any evergreen—big or small, fat or skinny, plastic or aluminum—the perfect tree.

TRIMMING THE TREE

The trimming of the tree is, in every home, an event. It would not be the same without a modicum of fussing, and the fussing begins with getting it to stand up straight. This is no small task, and one that requires years of careful study and technique honed by the owner of the legs seen sprawled beneath the lowest boughs. This individual will likely have a staunch and unyielding opinion about how, and with what, the tree should be watered. Best not to argue. Once the funny side—and every tree has one—has been turned to face the wall, the decorating begins.

It starts with the lights. In the same way that the carving of the Thanksgiving turkey is the duty of a very particular person, so is the task of stringing the lights. They have a gift, these people. Hand them a bird's nest of wires, and it comes untangled in their hands. They place each strand in such a way that when the lamps are dimmed, the tree twinkles like a starry night. Small children like to lie under the tree, gazing up with bright eyes that shine as if they can see all the way to heaven. Perhaps they can. Long ago, the flickering lights on Christmas trees came from the flames of candles, a symbol of the Light of the World, or the stars of heaven.

Boxes of ornaments are dug out of closets and attics and unpacked with great care and unapologetic nostalgia. The things that emerge from the tissue and bubble wrap are rediscovered every year, like treasures forgotten and found. In concert, they create a portrait of a family, a constellation of memories and a snapshot of style. The last flourish is the appointment of an angel, or a star, or the most special topper, upon the highest branch.

Trimmed Christmas trees are like snowflakes. Even in the same home, over the years no two are ever alike.

THE PEOPLE'S TREE

The National Christmas Tree gets our award for the most fussed-over tree in the South. The tradition of a community tree at the Capitol began in 1923, when President Calvin Coolidge pressed a button to illuminate 2,500 red, green, and white bulbs on a 45-foot balsam fir cut and erected near The Ellipse outside the White House. Thousands attended the grand illumination and joined church choirs and schoolchildren in singing carols for hours.

The following year, Coolidge decided against a cut tree, and asked for a live one to be planted and redecorated every year. But in 1929, an inspection of the tree revealed that the heat and weight of the Christmas lights had injured the tree. A new tree was replanted, and measures were taken to protect this one during the decorating process: Scaffolding was erected so ladders were not shoved in the branches; lighter-weight lights with lower voltage were used; and a fence was placed around the base to protect the fragile roots. The 1930 Grand Illumination went smoothly—until a fire broke out in the West Wing of the White House. It had to be gutted and rebuilt.

Subsequent trees have endured (or not) a succession of situations. A number of them have been damaged or killed by lights and decorations. Ornaments have been stolen. Lights have exploded. The star on top has shorted out. The train carrying a new tree has been derailed. Twice. Trees have been nearly uprooted, snapped in two by a windstorm, and blown over until they leaned like the Tower of Pisa. One was planted in haste before an approaching hurricane, deemed safer in the ground than on the back of a truck. In war years they have been left unlit to conserve power and observe security restrictions on outdoor lighting. They have been left dark to honor American hostages, and redecorated in January upon their return.

But not every year has seen a fiasco, and the National Community Christmas Tree (as it was renamed) has seen a number of lovely festivities and decorations. Trees have been accompanied by reindeer, jugglers, and clowns. They have been lit by solar power, LEDs, and blinking incandescents that used enough power to light two houses. They have been decorated with bows, suncatchers, holographic accents, snowflakes (that don't melt), sugarplums, kid-made ornaments, and a 4-foot red-and-green Liberty Bell. They have been presented to the President by a local Boy Scout and Girl Scout.

And all of them have been loved.

A TREE FOR ALL OF US

The holiday season officially begins December 7, when the President lights the 40-foot-tall Colorado spruce during the annual Pageant of Peace concert and tree-lighting ceremony. The National Park Service gives away a limited number of tickets for the event, but no worries if you're not in the area on the 7th—the tree stays lit throughout the season.

ANNUAL CHRISTMAS TREE HUNT

O' Christmas Tree . . . how lovely are your branches!

Let's gather at the Tree Farm
to find the perfect tree.

Dress: Cozy tartan attire
and warm boots

We'll end the day with a hearty picnic
in the pines!

A HEARTY
PICNIC
IN THE
PINES

Rosemary-Scented Cold Cider

Skillet Fried Chicken

Apple-Cabbage Slaw

Sweet Potato Salad

Chameleon Icebox Cookies

Caramel Drop-Banana Bread
Trifle Dessert

RECIPES ON PAGES 322-325

Skillet Fried Chicken

Caramel Drop-Banana Bread Trifle Dessert

CHRISTMAS SEASON TAILGATE FARE

Fetching a tree should not be done on an empty stomach. If you're headed to the woods or the Christmas tree farm, this make-ahead picnic travels well and tastes delicious cold. If your Christmas tree tradition involves a creaky ladder that unfolds from the ceiling with the tug of a string, we promise you'll enjoy it no less.

O CHRISTMAS TREE

RICK BRAGG

The Southern landscape, let's face it, is not intended for Christmas, at least not the storybook Christmas we cut out of red and green construction paper and taped to the windows at Roy Webb Elementary School. Most of the snowflakes I saw, until I left home, were frozen in place on a cardboard sky with Elmer's glue.

I do not love snow—I lived in Boston and New York and came to regard snow as a hard-packed, car-obscuring, finger-numbing, gray and dirty substance—but it was nice at Christmas till the snowplow came along and shoved it up over the top of your Subaru. Down here, I ride the highways and gaze out on the grass that has finally, grudgingly gone dormant, as the voices on the radio—Bing, Elvis, and them— try to assure me that it is indeed a time of white Christmas, and roasting chestnuts, and sleighs. And then a big ol' boy in a tank top and a Santy hat waves at me from his mailbox, and I am more confused.

That's when I see it, there at the side of the road: a single, perfectly shaped cedar or pine, not too short, not too tall, and I think, for just a second, that I wish I had a saw. And I know that, for me and mine, it is truly Christmas, after all.

There is no nice way to say it.

We are Christmas tree thieves, or used to be (though I am not ruling it out if I see just the right one outside a rest stop near Tupelo). I know that larceny has no place during Yuletide, and before you think badly of me, let me explain. It is not like we were rustling sheep from the manger scene in front of the city auditorium, or absconding with the Three Wise Men, which I think would be hard to pawn anyway. It was just trees. And in that we had scruples. We were not skulking through the lot at The Home Depot at three o'clock in the morning, or robbing a Douglas fir from the Knights of Columbus. It was just that we were less than particular about property lines.

When I was a child, we never bought a tree. We got an ax, or a handsaw, and went into the woods. It would have been a scene straight off a Christmas card, if we had actually gone hunting for one on our own land, which we did not have. I guess it was poaching in a way, but it seems harmless. In the deep woods, it was more like we were just thinning the herd, rather than stealing.

And, I doubt if a landowner ever walked up to a stump and said, "I'll see them Bragg boys swing for this." But we knew, my brothers and I, that there was something wrong about it.

So we decided to steal them from the State of Alabama. We would cruise the bigger roads and highways until we saw one on the state right-of-way. Sliding to a halt in the loose gravel, car tires smoking, I would leap from the truck with my ax. Three to six whacks would do it, unless I saw a car coming. Then I froze, trying to look innocent—with an ax in my hands.

That was a long time ago. I have not stolen a tree, from Alabama or anyone else, for 35 years. We buy our trees now, and pay what feels like $900 for a tree cut last Fourth of July, a tree I am afraid to shake too hard, lest it look like something Charlie Brown would have. You got a much better quality of tree, when it was stole.

But I am too old and stiff now, too fat to jump a ditch or climb a bank. The police would get me, sure, and my wife would not come and bail me out until after New Year's, perhaps Easter.

Still I see them there, at the side of the road in that balmy air, and it makes me happy.

I guess, to be truthful, those stuck-on paper snowflakes did, too.

DECKING

THE

HALLS

The wreath is the gateway decor to more enthusiastic
ornamentation. It soon leads to a broad sweep of garland
draped over the doorway. Then the garland gets enhanced
with pinecones, velvety ribbons, and glass bulbs until it can hold
no more. That paves the way for twin topiaries, strung with white
lights or studded with winter citrus. The next thing you know, you
have dozens of wreaths, one for each window, and the porch has
become its own ecosystem, like a life-size bell jar garden.

PORCHES

AND

FRONT DOORS

Many of us are as particular about our holiday foliage as we are about our interior design. We complement our architecture. We embrace local foliage and regional style. We elevate the objects we find all around us: oyster shells and palmettos in the Lowcountry; prickly pear cactus in Texas; Spanish moss and succulents on the Florida coast. Like a local accent, these regional details lend an only-here authenticity.

The combination produces in each part of the South a singular look—and a universal pride of place. Charleston's grand Victorians are draped with pine garlands and accented with pineapples, a symbol of hospitality. Asheville's Craftsman bungalows are dressed in North Carolina Fraser fir and rustic details—pinecones and birds' nests, feathers and twigs—in place of flashy ribbon. In Williamsburg, tailored boxwood wreaths with red velvet bows put the finishing touch on white Colonials, like a classic accessory. Victorians on New Orleans' Canal Street overflow with fussy bows and fancy glass bulbs. Standing on the sidewalk before these homes, dressed in their holiday finest, it is impossible to question where you are.

And then there are the lights.

This is one of those topics that, like liquor and the Iron Bowl, divides us into fiercely opposing camps. All white or color. Twinkling or steady. Strung on the house or on bushes and trees—at least 200 bulbs per vertical foot. Luminarias. Candles. Spotlights on the trees. December's days are the shortest of the year. We must brighten them any way we know how.

A SOUTHERN WELCOME

A 1905 Maryland home, built during the transition between the Queen Anne and the Colonial Revival architectural styles, offers a warm reception to all. The century-old 4-foot-wide front door and 8-foot-wide front porch convey comfort and elegance—the ultimate expression of Southern hospitality at Christmastime and beyond.

ILLUMINATING
THE SEASON

You either swear by all-white lights or pledge your devotion to color. There is no middle ground. We shall argue neither side. We say only: Let there be lights! Lots of lights.

SETTING THE SCENE

Like a well-chosen party invitation, the things you hang on your home with love make a memorable first impression. They set a tone and hint deliciously at the wonders that await inside.

WARM RECEPTION

Whether the guests standing on your porch are carolers, family members arriving from out of town, or friends dropping by for a visit, they will lose themselves for a moment in the environment you have created.

WREATHS

In the most barren of seasons, the act of bringing greenery inside is a luxury that celebrates the gifts of nature. As we search our landscape for lovely living things to bring inside, we are forced to look past the bleakness of winter and see what thrives despite it. Evergreens embody the persistence of life and the promise of warm months to come. We embellish our homes with found beauty, foraged or plucked, filling our rooms with the ebullient freshness of the outdoors.

The tradition of holiday greenery dates back thousands of years to ancient winter festivals long before the dawn of Christianity. These traditions were later adopted into religious holidays, and adapted with a blend of old and new meaning that continues to resonate. Cedar signifies strength and healing. The laurel represents victory over suffering and persecution. Pine is a symbol of immortality. Pinecones, nuts, and seeds are signs of life and resurrection. Prickly holly is particularly rich with Christian symbolism: sharp leaves that evoke the crown of thorns, red berries bright as blood.

While today's wreaths may or may not hold the same meaning, their execution has evolved into something akin to fashion. Some of us have childhood memories of making our own wreaths, cutting Muscadine vines growing wild in the woods with a Buck knife. We twined it into a circle—the base of the wreath—and filled it out with feathery tufts of red cedar. Red cedar isn't a cedar, of course, but a juniper that grows all over the South, from Lowcountry marshes to Appalachian hillsides. Spirited from roadsides and backyards, it makes a fine wreath. When it grows tall enough, and your budget is slim, it also makes a fine Christmas tree.

But we find no shame in a store-bought wreath, embellished with things we gather and cut to make them beautifully original: dried hydrangeas saved from summer's bumper crop; fresh citrus from the farmers' market; fragrant rosemary from the otherwise dormant garden; wild berries found in the woods. Our signature touch may be last year's dried magnolia leaves spray-painted gold for some festive bling. Or maybe the wreath has no green at all—just one big explosion of ribbon declaring our favorite football team, or a cluster of glass bulbs in a color palette that hints at the wonders beyond the door.

A CIRCLE OF WELL WISHES

Wreaths, like statement jewelry custom-made for your front door, project a message and a sense of style. As classic or elaborate as you wish, they are a public greeting to passersby, a warm welcome to friends and neighbors, and the last thing a guest sees before crossing the threshold into your home. As is evidenced on the following pages, the South is blessed with an abundance of natural materials that lend themselves to the creation of wreaths that are beautifully unique to the area's various regions.

Fine mornings are spent getting Christmas trees from the woods, in making holly wreaths and hanging up mistletoe boughs. The days are golden with sunshine, the forests glowing with color. Everywhere there is fulfillment of last spring's promise. Black walnuts and hickory nuts drop with emphatic thuds; chinquapins fall from dry burs and hide under their own fallen leaves; under live-oaks, water-oaks, Spanish oaks, the earth is covered with acorns, yet the chestnut-oaks drop their loads of big overcups in a steady patter. The magnolias are green and glossy, mock oranges glisten in the sun light, Cherokee-rose apples shine among the glossy leaves.

—JULIA PETERKIN, *A Plantation Christmas*

ENTRYWAYS
AND
LIVING ROOMS

If the outside of the house is the opening monologue, the inside is the stage for the joyful drama that unfurls throughout the holidays. The atmosphere we create with well-orchestrated details—a deliberate medley of color, texture, sound, and scent—infuses every moment we spend inside. We take great care to get it all just right, because this scene becomes the backdrop for our memories.

As our guests take their first steps into our home, we want them not only to see, but also feel. Wonder. Peace. Comfort. Joy. Most of all, we want them to feel welcome. Our entryway greets them with garland festooned with bright ribbon or poinsettias marching up the staircase or topiaries or children or dogs in a space that comes to life in every sense. The scent of a candle layers over the aroma of pine, cut by a fleeting sweet breath of paperwhites. The warmth of our home embraces them as they hand us their coats and leave the cold behind.

A good decorator knows that details matter. Like the modest ingredients of flour, salt, yeast, and water transform into the magic of bread, the tiniest details create an atmosphere that transcends the mere sum of its parts. Every room is a kaleidoscope of these details, set in contrast to great effect. The tender stalks and bright blooms of amaryllis appear more delicate against a backdrop of hardy evergreens. A jar of red and white peppermints is brighter and sweeter when set off by dark cedar.

THE JOY OF THE SEASON

When the last wreath has been hung and the mess cleaned up, we will step back and behold a transformation that, year after year, still catches our breath.

NATIVE SPLENDOR

The aroma of native greenery greets
guests with a fresh welcome, whether
it's delicately scented boxwood wreaths
on the banister or a lavishly decorated
garland of cedar and pine.

Hospitality is a Southern specialty, one that makes itself known especially at Christmas. A table full of good food continues to be the centerpiece of festivities, but now the entry hall is decorated with flowers and greenery, setting the stage for celebrations.

Holiday decorations express not only time-honored traditions but unconventional style, making every Christmas tree and every wrapped gift a from-the-heart expression of the season.

"Each year, I invite my friends and family to trim the tree. I have big bushels of red, green, yellow, and white ornaments. Everyone divides into groups and we decorate the 12-foot tree. We don't give gifts; we just give the gift of being together."

—MAYA ANGELOU

EVERY TREE TELLS A STORY

An inky handprint on a construction-paper star, a reindeer with pipe-cleaner antlers, a delicate blue bell with
a tarnished silver clapper—such treasures, lovingly unwrapped and hung in place, transform tree branches into
storytellers that year after year impart a family's history and holiday traditions.

ODE TO THE
HOMEMADE ORNAMENT

KIM CROSS

It's not Christmas until we hang the silver blob.

The most beloved ornament on our tree, it is a Rorschach test of metal, like a soldering project gone wrong, hung by a white pipe cleaner that has seen better days. It is a forlorn, pitiful-looking thing. It brings me great mirth and joy.

I never hang the blob on the wall side of the tree. It goes on the front, surrounded by prettier things, which only make it look more like an orphan. I hang it right about eye level, so guests can see it and wonder. Because if they are not too polite, they will ask.

And then I get to tell The Story.

Our tree is not trimmed with ornaments. Our branches are filled with stories. They do not match. They are colorful, but they adhere to no palette. In this era of trees with decorator palettes, ours is a merry mess, a hodgepodge of memories that we get to relive every year.

The storytelling begins with the ceremonial unpacking of a great plastic tub retrieved from the attic, out of which we pull out fistfuls of wrinkled tissue paper and yellowed bubble wrap. The last 11 months have over-written our memory of what is inside, so it feels like unwrapping a gift. Most of the contents make us smile. Some of them make us shake our heads and laugh. One of them makes my husband roll his eyes and sigh deeply.

We usually start with the seashells. They're not really shells but fragments of shells, crushed by the waves of a distant sea and then tumbled in the restless surf until the sharp edges were polished round. Each handful of mother-of-pearl, hot-glue-gunned to a cheap piece of twine, takes me back to that distant shore—the first big trip I took with the man I would marry.

And then I am standing in our first apartment, the one with a magnificent view but no couch or TV. We splurged on a fresh tree for our first Christmas, but ornaments were not in our budget. I did not feel deprived. We didn't have much, but we had a hot-glue gun. More than a decade later, that mother-of-pearl still shines brighter than anything I have ever seen in a store.

Next we hang the pewter heart engraved with our wedding date. We laugh about the sudden gust of wind that tossed my veil on his head, our appropriately cheesy handwritten vows, and Grandma's comment, caught on camera as we walked away married: "Well that was unusual!"

After that comes a felt-framed photo of our son, born two days after Christmas. The hospital sent him home in a stocking sewn by sweet old ladies. We bring that out, too, and make him hold it for a photo. We plan to do this every year, until we have to hold his car keys hostage.

Then comes the tiny handprint on a small glass bulb that gets hung as high as possible. The candy-cane reindeer with pipe-cleaner antlers and googly eyes. The finger-painted train. We watch the handprints grow through the years. Dreams sketched in crayon and tempura paint become identifiable. Misspellings diminish and handwriting assumes better posture. Faces framed in felt grow older.

We add a new chapter to our tree every year. Last year, my mother gave me the plaster of Paris handprint that I made for her in kindergarten. My 5-year-old son placed his hand in it, and it fit. I got kind of weepy.

And then I remembered The Blob.

Suddenly I am standing in the old apartment, back in our no-couch days, when making tea was a daily luxury, though we didn't own a kettle. It is cold, and I come home to a quiet apartment with a strange, metallic odor. It smells like something is burning.

In the kitchen, I see it: a pot on fire. Flames flicker where the water should be. I grab a towel and lift it from the stove, and the bottom melts right off. I did not know that pots could melt. When it cools and hardens in a shiny silver puddle, I smile and grab a pipe cleaner. I find my husband in the basement, lost in some project. I hold it up and ask him if he wants some tea.

His face goes white as snow. 🎋

MANTELS

Few holiday decorations evoke the Southern ethos like a fireplace mantel overflowing with a lush garland of magnolia. Our most iconic evergreen is associated with beauty and dignity. The state flower of Mississippi, magnolia grows wild in many states and is a favorite of landscapers and decorators. Its glossy green leaves are beautiful fresh or dried, and their velveteen undersides lend texture and contrast. It pairs beautifully with wood or brick, and never goes out of style.

The same can be said of mistletoe. Though not strictly Southern, this funny little plant has shallow roots in the tops of trees and deep roots in legend and folklore. Once gathered for ancient midwinter festivals, it was considered a token of peace, and that meaning carried over when it was adopted by Christians and used to decorate churches. The custom of stealing a kiss under the mistletoe developed in medieval English homes, where believers hung an effigy of the holy family in a wooden hoop decorated with evergreens. This evolved into a "kissing bough" of mixed evergreens that included mistletoe. For every kiss, a berry was removed. When all the berries were gone, so were the kisses.

A different species from the English mistletoe, our version is easy to spot in winter, a lonely bright splotch of green hiding in the tops of bare deciduous trees. Our hunters still harvest it with the great Southern method of shooting it out of the treetops in the middle of a winter hunt.

As we swag the mantel and trim the tree, our home becomes a winter garden where we gather with the people we love. But for now we fight a bird's nest of Christmas lights, or look for the bulb that shorted the strand, and hang the fragile ornaments well out of the littlest one's reach.

NATURE'S ORNAMENTS

The South's temperate climate lends itself to an abundance of natural materials that Southerners have long
looked to for holiday embellishments. Chief among them are fresh magnolia, Fraser fir, and boxwood,
with pinecones and berry branches adding festive trimmings.

Sometimes the prettiest holiday mantel decorations can also be the simplest. The classic greenery-laden mantel with the sweet scents of nature is somehow always appropriate—like an expensive perfume.

TRIMMED WITH LOVE

The mantel, the most decorated sliver of real estate in the living room, gives a place of importance to treasured keepsakes and collections, reinforcing the ties between fond memories and holiday trimmings.

HOLIDAY
BLOOMS

We have a Southerner to thank for introducing the poinsettia to America: a Charlestonian named Joel Roberts Poinsett. A congressman who became the first U.S. ambassador to Mexico, Poinsett fell in love with the painted-leaf plant during his official sojourn south of the border in the 1820s. He also happened to be an avid botanist, and the clippings he cultivated in his Charleston greenhouse thrived under his expert care. Poinsett gave them as gifts to family and friends, and this early Southern pass-along plant became a nationwide icon of Christmas. Congress even designated December 12 as Poinsettia Day to honor Poinsett's red-and-green thumb.

Like the mistletoe, the poinsettia is steeped in legend. Some say the plant's green leaves turned red when a woman separated from her lover on Christmas Eve died of heartbreak. Another legend holds that the Star of Bethlehem turned the poinsettia's green leaves to the color of fire as it shone brightly on the night before Jesus was born. One story tells of a Mexican peasant too poor to afford a Christmas offering for the altar. He fell to his knees to pray for guidance, and when he rose, the first Flores de Noche Buena, "Flowers of the Holy Night," sprang up from the spot where he knelt.

In our desire to surround ourselves with beauty, we have learned to trick some living things into blooming out of season for our pleasure. It is a symbiotic relationship. We force them to bloom. They force us to stop at least once a day, captivated by their beauty.

The amaryllis blooms in the heart of winter, emerging with the self-possession of a debutante pretending not to notice her command over every eye in the room. As she grows, she unfurls before your eyes, mocking the dark eternity of December. A little coquette, she loves being the center of attention in a room, and flaunts her beauty shamelessly.

Paperwhites are the Melanie to the scarlet amaryllis. Pure and white, their subtle beauty draws less attention but infuses the air around them with a pleasant sweetness. They poke their heads out of the rocks shyly and bloom in earnest. Like the evergreens, these beauties defy winter. But they are delicate and ephemeral, a reminder of the fleeting nature of Nature and seasons that never stop changing. We give them as a gift that gives a little more every day. To watch them grow is to be aware of the passing of time, to appreciate this gift called the present.

Every year around this time, the keepers of an heirloom Christmas cactus bring out a small potted plant that looks plain and unassuming for most of the year, but is about to burst into fireworks. This succulent—it's not a true cactus—spends most of the year parked on the sunny side of the porch or forgotten in some corner. But as the holiday grows near, it seems to sense it is time to celebrate. At the end of its long and segmented leaves, tender flowers unfurl in cheerful colors—pink, white, red, orange, or purple.

"This was my grandmother's Christmas cactus," the keepers will say, showing it off with unrestrained nostalgia. "I grew it from a cutting."

We say "keepers," because you never really own a Christmas cactus; you simply take care of it for the next generation. The tender-looking succulent is a treasured Southern plant tough enough to outlive most pets and handed down through generations. Luckily, its cuttings are easy to propagate—a wise option for keepers with multiple heirs.

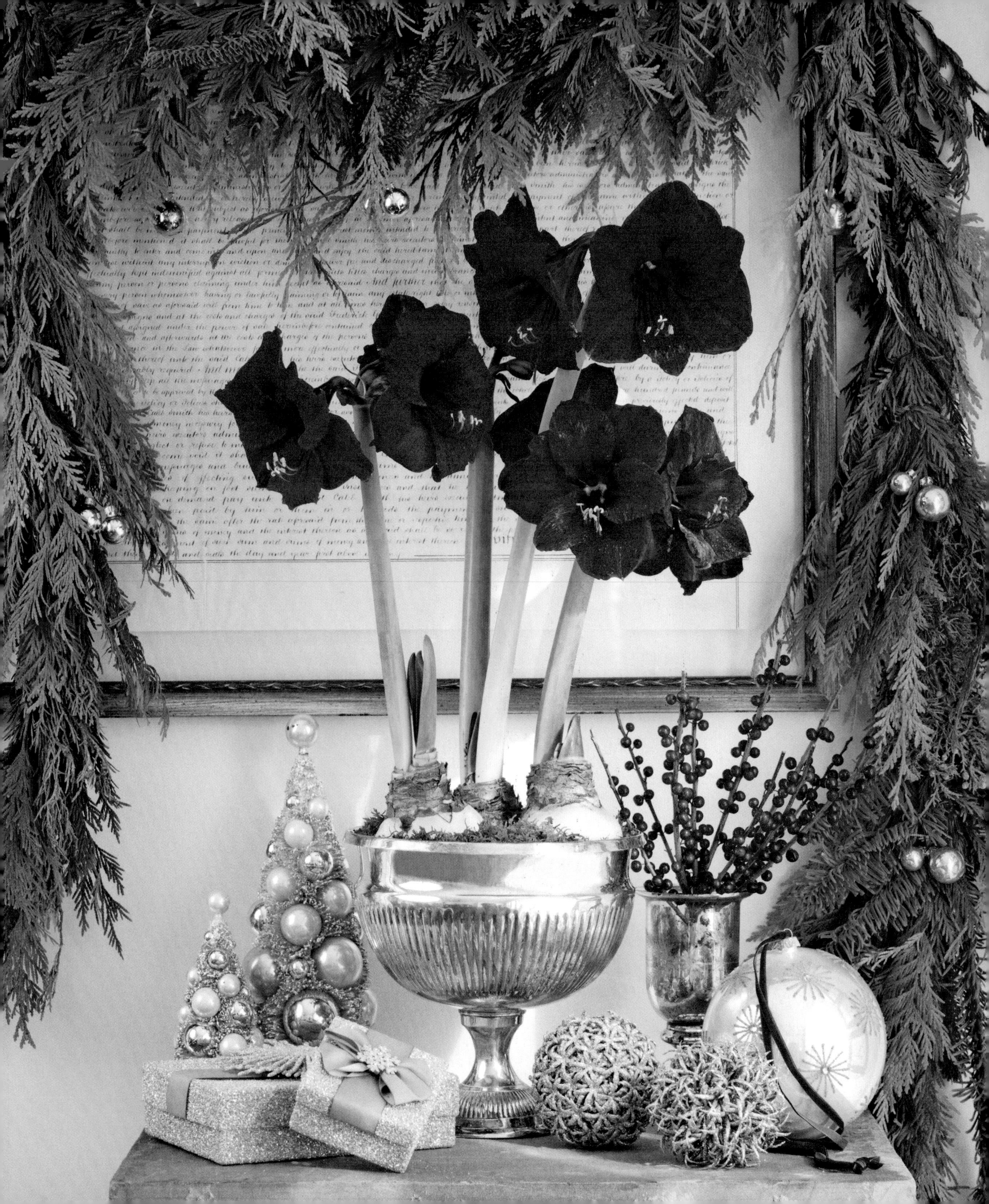

In the handsome room, in artificial light, the amaryllis seemed to have taken on glamour, like a beautiful girl all dressed up for the evening. All dressed up and no place to go, he thought . . . The amaryllis was different, entirely. He liked just being with it. Because of its size, he supposed, it seemed to have individuality, and then he had watched it grow daily, with his naked eye. Looking at the blooms, he thought of words like pure and noble, and old lines of poetry like "Euclid alone has looked on Beauty bare."

—MARY WARD BROWN, "The Amaryllis"

Share Some Christmas Cheer

Celebrate the season
at a casual cocktail supper
followed by caroling around
the piano.

Saturday, December 6

7:00 p.m.

A CASUAL COCKTAIL SUPPER

Perfect Beef Tenderloin with
Homemade Hot Mustard
and Horseradish Sauce

Montgomery Punch

Cheese Dreams

Asparagus with Curry Dip

Mini Corn Cakes with Smoked
Salmon and Dill Crème Fraîche

Lump Crab Mornay

Cheese Spread

Buttery Toasted Pecans

Pecan Bourbon Balls

RECIPES ON PAGES 326-329

Perfect Beef
Tenderloin with Home-
made Hot Mustard and
Horseradish Sauce

Montgomery Punch

Mini Corn Cakes with Smoked Salmon and Dill
Crème Fraîche, Cheese Dreams

Asparagus with Curry Dip

Lump Crab Mornay

Buttery Toasted Pecans,
Cheese Spread

FESTIVE FAVORITES

A cocktail supper featuring classic Southern dishes is the perfect start to the season. With a decades-old
Mississippi recipe for Homemade Hot Mustard; Montgomery Punch, a town staple; and must-have Cheese
Dreams and Pecan Bourbon Balls, the party is complete.

Pecan Bourbon Balls

COCKTAIL SUPPER

JULIA REED

I love giving parties at Christmas, mainly because the guests are already in the mood to make merry. They're primed to blow off their diets and imbibe more than usual, they want to dress up and show off, and they're not embarrassed to stick holly in their hair. There's also the convenient fact that the halls—and the mantels and the table—have all been decked (in my case with piles of gorgeous seasonal citrus and branches from the magnolia just outside). Which leads us to my favorite form of holiday entertainment, the Cocktail Supper, a big boozy bash with enough food to constitute supper that's also the perfect marriage of party and season.

My mother is a lifelong proponent of the Cocktail Supper, an event I copied and have been forced to explain ever since, especially during my years in New York, where people were not just confused but slightly terrified by the term. ("Can we just stop by, or do we have to sit down?" "Are you only serving cocktails, or shall we bring wine?" "What does supper mean, exactly?") The irony is that it's the most forgiving of formats—for the guests as well as the hosts. The menu items are designed to be eaten easily and relatively neatly with your hands, which means that the real progress of a party—visiting, drinking, flirting, meeting new people, or making a quick escape—is not hindered by the pesky tasks of fixing a plate, juggling utensils, and finding a place to perch. And as the host, your job is simple: Keep the bar and the table replenished, and everything else—dancing, impromptu caroling, illicit sessions under real or imagined mistletoe—takes care of itself.

Over the years, I've tweaked my mother's standby menu only slightly. There's always a platter of rare, room-temperature tenderloin on the table (though her homemade yeast rolls have been replaced, mercifully, by Sister Schubert's fine facsimiles) along with a rich Lump Crab Mornay, kept warm by the underused wonder that is a silver chafing dish. In a bow to something green, I offer up steamed asparagus with curry dip, a mildly spicy, garlicky concoction I've only ever encountered in the Mississippi Delta, where I grew up. Then there's smoked salmon on miniature cornbread muffins rather than the usual blini or brown bread.

To further enhance the flow, I pass one or two hot hors d'oeuvres. (My grandmother's addictive, make-ahead cheese dreams are always huge hits.) If you have a piano, hire someone to play it, and be sure to put nibbles nearby. (Roasted pecans and a Roquefort spread inspired by Julia Child work nicely.) Finally, nothing is more festive on a sideboard than a big bowl of Champagne punch, especially when adorned with a pretty ice ring. As for something sweet, you cannot beat classic bourbon balls dressed in a coat of those same salty pecans that accompany the Roquefort—they'll also help the children sleep more soundly.

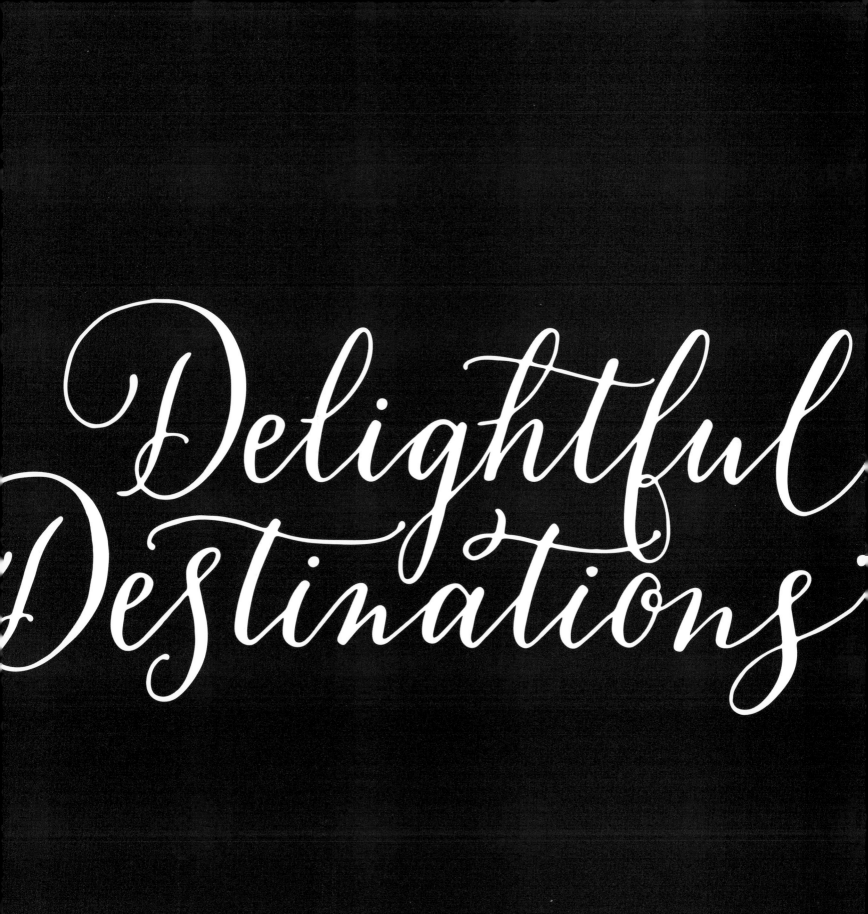

Delightful
Destinations

DELIGHTFUL
DESTINATIONS

In this glad season, we have first focused on our homes and, guided by our family's traditions, have covered every last celebratory detail. We can finally exhale with our houses perfectly trimmed in evergreens, ribbons, and baubles. We have been peering inside figuratively as well, cloaking ourselves with introspection, examining our beliefs and joys and all the memories that surface with the approaching holidays.

And now we can begin to look outside—outside of ourselves and outside of our homes. We can truly venture out to revel in the sights and sounds of Christmas.

It begins with a simple walk down the block to view the delicate string light swags on our neighbors' front porches. From there it progresses further into the community. It is the pilgrimage to that house in town that blankets each of its own square feet with blinking lights and fills its lawn with all manner of motorized sleighs led by deer, navigated by elves, and captained by Jolly Old Saint Nicholas.

It is huddling in shoulder to shoulder with neighbors to watch the town's Christmas parade as it marches down Main Street. The high school band in starched uniforms sends brassy notes into the crisp winter air, beating to its own rump-a-pum-pum. Waving from the back of the polished, brand-new or classically old convertibles are the darling queens: the Catfish Queen, or Little Miss Insert-Your-Local-Crop-Here, her title spelled out with glitter on a satin sash. Tiny dancers in patent leather shoes tap rhythms across the cold asphalt, or bounce rubber balls spray-painted white to look like snowballs. Children open their small hands, and like chirping baby birds, yell, "Candy! Candy!" and are graciously rewarded with a light rain of suckers and treats—pitter, patter, pitter, patter—in cinnamon and peppermint flavors. And, of course, there is Santa again—he always comes to our parade—except now he's riding on the biggest, reddest, shiniest fire truck the department owns.

It is the stroll by the department stores' decadent window displays that closely resemble art installations. It is the homes tours and neighborhood Open House celebrations, those opportunities to pique our curiosity about how others celebrate and simultaneously gather new decorating ideas. It is the cozy inns and ornate hotels and fine restaurants that pull out all the stops and create picture-postcard scenes this time of year especially for us, the visitors.

Because sharing Christmas, with others in other places, fosters our community connections and enhances our entire, season-long celebration.

Here's an idea that may sound strange to you. What if you throw all the Christmas Day traditions out the window one year? Instead of the family shuffle—a visit with this side of grandparents for 2.75 hours before quickly rushing to that side of grandparents for 2.75 hours—you change the whole game and start a new tradition, your own tradition: a Christmas Travel Trip.

Perhaps you make Christmas Eve or Day reservations at a swanky hotel. Perhaps it's three or four days overnight in a place you've only read about. Once there, you will quickly realize you are not alone. Lots of couples and families claim these trips as their ideal Christmas.

Of course, you'll still be connected. You'll make those phone calls to both grandmas' houses and sit patiently while the phone is passed around to capture the babies cooing, your mom describing every dish and dishing about every piece if gossip, your dad with his lovable grunts, and your siblings who are still scratching their heads at how you took off on your own adventure. Because that's exactly what it's going to be. An adventure.

And what's wonderful about the South is that it is ripe with adventure around the holidays. There are endless possibilities for destinations to explore. One place to start is by discovering all the varied seasonal traditions our region shares. Other states may claim the biggest Christmas store, or the tallest tree, or the most electrifying display of lights. But nowhere else can you find the distinct cultural mix of traditions observed across the South.

EXCITING EXCURSIONS

Spectacular decorations and seasonal activities at resort getaways will enchant the whole family and may even forge new Christmas traditions. Savage River Lodge, which is surrounded by about 750 acres of the Savage River State Forest, promises a relaxing respite from the holiday bustle. Landmarks in Savannah, though always beautiful, are made even more so with the addition of sparkling trimmings.

Savage River Lodge
Frostburg, Maryland

Savannah, Georgia

Savannah, Georgia

It is the glad season.

Thunder ebbs to silence and lightning sleeps quietly
in the corner.

Flood waters recede into memory.

Snow becomes a yielding cushion to aid us

as we make our way to higher ground.

Hope is born again in the faces of children

It rides on the shoulders of our aged as they walk
into their sunsets.

Hope spreads around the earth. Brightening all things,

Even hate which crouches breeding in dark corridors.

In our joy, we think we hear a whisper.

At first it is too soft. Then only half heard.

We listen carefully as it gathers strength.

We hear a sweetness.

The word is peace.

It is loud now. It is louder.

Louder than the explosion of bombs.

—MAYA ANGELOU, excerpted from
"Amazing Peace: A Christmas Poem"

SIGHTS

AND

SOUNDS

As the holiday season becomes increasingly crowded with fake trees and subpar mall Santas, it's impossible not to yearn for some authenticity. You don't have to venture far to find a lovably genuine small-town Christmas parade, but across the South there are parades, light tours, and getaways that reflect the unique character of the South's distinctive regions.

PARADES

Everyone has a favorite spot, the perfect perch or vantage point, to watch the Christmas parade. Maybe it's early enough in the route where the marchers are still excited, even slightly nervous, as they perform their routines. While your toes dangle off the curb, all around you, proud papas shoulder their kids who applaud giddily at every floats' detail and the bellowing laughter and well-wishes from Santa, the annual, de facto grand marshal.

Folks in the Old Dominion have been celebrating Christmas for centuries, and they still know how to throw a party when December rolls around. In Middleburg, the unmistakable headliners of Middleburg's Hunt Review Parade are the dozens of frisky hounds marching down Main Street on the brisk and wintry first Saturday in December. They are followed closely by horse-mounted riders clad in red and representing the fox hunting tradition that has helped to define this small Virginia town since 1905. The Middleburg Hunt was started, quite simply, to settle a bet over whether English or American hounds were the better hunters. Incidentally, the American hounds won the first match, and the town has revered the hunts ever since. History is no stranger to this village, first settled in 1787, and you can experience it for yourself in the homes, inns, restaurants, and antiques shops that draw visitors any time of year to this region of the state that has also gained notoriety for its vineyards and wineries. But this family-friendly holiday parade—with its marching bands, carolers, and Santa in a carriage drawn by Ayrshire horses—marks one of the most special times for Middleburg.

RIDING TO HOUNDS

Mounted riders, sleek horses, and 80 happy hounds lead the grand Hunt Review Parade in Middleburg, an 18th-century village in the heart of Virginia's Hunt Country.

Christmas at Williamsburg is wrapped in simplicity and the warm glow of centuries-old traditions. The music of fifes and drums can be heard everywhere during the season.

In the re-created Colonial capital of Virginia, Christmas traditions live on. Costumed interpreters create beautiful, seasonal music by caroling, or playing instruments—the drums and flutes. This is the time for what they call the Grand Illumination, when candles flicker in the windows of centuries-old homes and line the cupolas like lanterns. Virtually every building in the historic area stands dressed in holiday attire—fresh fruit and woodland foliage hang from doors. Here, we can't help but be reminded of our heritage, of the celebrations enjoyed by our founding fathers and mothers.

Indeed, the decorations alone are worth a visit to Williamsburg at Christmas. Apples, pineapples, oranges, lemons, pears, pinecones, acorns, and nuts of every kind gleam from their nests amid the leaves of pine and holly. The most beautiful decorations can be seen from the street. Inside, they are minimal, in keeping with the practice of Colonial times, where Christmas was more a holy day than a holiday.

A bit farther south along Alabama's Gulf Coast, parades move from streets to waterways as boats festooned with colorful lights proceed east down the Intracoastal Canal Waterway to Orange Beach in a floating flotilla. With most of the surfaces wrapped in string lights, the vessels in this parade resemble floating lanterns. The event is a decades-long tradition along the coast, and it's open to everyone and free to enter. No boat? No problem. You can rent one from a local marina.

FESTIVE FLOTILLA

For the past 28 years, coastal Alabama boat captains have lined up their crafts for one of the area's favorite holiday events, the Annual Christmas Lighted Boat Parade.

Virginia Beach, Virginia

"On a sleigh, I dreamed, I could glide carefree across the ice, and, with the proper number of tiny reindeer, even fly across the world."

— RICK BRAGG

SEASIDE CELEBRATION

Holiday events such as caroling and parade watching naturally generate gatherings of friends and family. In anticipation of an evening boat parade, a Gulf-side home is the ideal setting for a casual supper.

While in the area, you'll want to visit the sweet little beach towns that dot the shoreline like precious charms on a bracelet. If you're cruising that way, you'll be pleasantly thankful that you have to slow down while passing through places like Grayton Beach, WaterColor, Seaside, Seagrove, Alys Beach, Rosemary Beach, and on and on.

Throughout the holiday season, each one of these communities celebrates in its own unique way with decorative displays and classical music concerts. Christmas down along the Gulf Coast feels a little different than elsewhere in the South. With average highs in the mid 60s, any snow has to be man-made. And guess what? At WaterColor's Old Florida Holiday and Winter Market, you'll see it swirling through the air.

This celebration, usually held toward the end of November, features local vendors, artists, and crafters. Horses draw carriages that clop, clop, clop around Cerulean Park. Locals toast marshmallows at fire pits. Santa sits perched on a beach chair. And the wassail flows freely.

When visiting, you must stroll back into the side streets to check out the homes, many of which feature simple clapboard exteriors and light, airy palettes (think white, turquoise, and apple green) that mirror the laid-back lifestyle and architecture of the community.

COASTAL CHRISTMAS

Decorating a seaside cottage for Christmas doesn't mean forgoing tradition. With a few creative spins, the holiday trimmings can reflect the sand and surf while preserving seasonal conventions.

BRIGHT CHRISTMAS

The light, airy palette and native materials echo the sand and sea and convey
Christmas with a seaside vibe.

Holiday Supper
by the Sea

——◆——

By land or by sea, stop by for
a before-the-parade meal.

What to bring: binoculars for
watching the boat parade
on the coast

SUPPER
BY THE SEA

Orange Thing Punch

Benne Seed Cheese Wafers

Shrimp and Andouille Sausage
over Parmesan Grits

Garlic Roasted Asparagus

White Chocolate-Cranberry
Crème Brûlée

RECIPES ON PAGES 330-332

Benne Seed Cheese Wafers,
Orange Thing Punch

Shrimp and Andouille Sausage over Parmesan Grits,
Garlic Roasted Asparagus

White Chocolate-Cranberry
Crème Brûlée

It was a four-hundred-mile trip, something like that. My first stop was in Mobile. I changed buses there, and rode along forever and forever through swampy lands and along seacoasts until we arrived in a loud city tinkling with trolley cars and packed with dangerous foreign-looking people. That was New Orleans.

And suddenly, as I stepped off the bus, a man swept me in his arms, squeezed the breath out of me; he was laughing, he was crying—a tall, good-looking man, laughing and crying. He said: "Don't you know me? Don't you know your daddy?"

I was speechless. I didn't say a word until at last, when we were riding along in a taxi, I asked: "Where is it?"

"Our house? It's not far—"

"Not the house. The snow."

"What snow?"

"I thought there would be a lot of snow."

He looked at me strangely, but laughed. "There never has been any snow in New Orleans. Not that I heard of. But listen. Hear that thunder? It's sure going to rain!"

—TRUMAN CAPOTE, "One Christmas"

The Homestead
Hot Springs, Virginia

SEASONAL
SITES

Some of the South's most iconic destinations dress themselves in their best finery at the holidays. Before the family nestles at home for a Christmas holiday celebration, the weeks leading up to the big day are the perfect time to escape to the wonders of the season around the South.

A good place to consider is a spot where every day is a celebration. Whether it's a jazz brunch, a backyard crawfish boil, or a flurry of flying beads at Mardi Gras, it's well established that the good folks in Louisiana know how to celebrate. Christmas is no exception. Rowdy, rustic, and robustly seasoned, Cajun Country revels in the holidays with its own accordion-fueled beat. In addition to the region's iconic pleasures—fiery gumbo, zydeco music—December brings spirited festivals, historic churches cloaked in twinkly lights, and antebellum mansions decked in Victorian finery that offer new ways to appreciate the region's rich culture. Even Papa Noel, the fabled Cajun Santa, arrives in rustic style with a party in the woods.

Jingling bells take on a decidedly zydeco beat when you hear them in Lafayette during the holidays. This south-central Louisiana city is a must-see during this time of year. Just south of Lafayette, Acadian Village, a quaint replica of an 1800s town, welcomes visitors all year long, but Christmas brings lots of special events. Among the houses and businesses, some built as early as 1790, there are animated light displays, a carousel and train ride for the children, and Christmas arts and crafts for holiday gift giving.

Dusk is the perfect time to arrive at Acadian Village, which is a bit like the Disney version of ye olde Louisiana. It is named for the Acadians, descendants of French colonists who settled in this area of the state and developed what we now know as Cajun culture. The majority of the buildings in this village were originally authentic homes donated by the families whose ancestors built them. Each has been renovated and displays details from the lives of those early settlers.

Around the holidays, it transforms into Noël Acadian au Village, where each evening in December, more than a half million lights illuminate the buildings. Particularly notable areas for lights include The New Chapel, the blacksmith shop, restored cypress cottages, and a paddle-boat cloaked in colored bulbs. Local Cajun bands, hot pork jambalaya, and carnival rides round out the revelry.

Noël Acadian au Village
near Lafayette, Louisiana

Jackson Square
New Orleans, Louisiana

SPARKLE IN THE CITY

Locals and visitors alike hum and sing as they make their way through the French Quarter for the free Caroling at Jackson Square. And, just about everyone in town takes at least one lingering walk along the marble floors of the swank, block-long lobby of The Roosevelt Hotel to revel in its fantastic display of trees and twinkling white lights.

The Roosevelt Hotel
New Orleans, Louisiana

Johnson City, Texas

Riverwalk
San Antonio, Texas

IN THE HEART OF TEXAS

It's said that everything's bigger in Texas, and each year, deep in the Hill Country, several communities set out to prove it, illuminating themselves by wrapping lights around anything they can find—public structures, trees, shrubs. None, however, matches the scope of Johnson City (birthplace of President Lyndon B. Johnson), though San Antonio's Riverwalk comes close.

MOUNTAIN TRADITIONS

Blackberry Farm
Walland, Tennessee

Williamsburg, Virginia

In the eastern region of the South, the Appalachians preserve folk tales as colorful as they are old. Some mountain dwellers continued for generations to celebrate "Old Christmas" on January 6, the date observed until 1752, when the Gregorian calendar replaced the Julian calendar and gave us December 25. All sorts of magnificent phenomena are believed to occur on Old Christmas. Bees are said to swarm out of the hive at midnight and hum the Hundredth Psalm until dawn. Water turns to wine at the stroke of midnight, when animals everywhere kneel to honor the birth of the baby king. It is good luck to hear the chirp of a cricket in the hearth on Christmas Eve, and even luckier to be born on Christmas Day.

The area where this charming lore dwells is also home to a wonderland of luxurious getaways that pampers the heart and the soul at Christmastime. Such a place is Blackberry Farm in Walland, Tennessee, where the rolling Smoky Mountain landscape provides a lush, romantic backdrop for the hotel's famous farmhouse-chic vibe.

For Old World traditions, look no further than Colonial Williamsburg, an area of the South that's distinguished by a rich history, and where, at holiday time, a single candle burns in each window of historic homes older than our country. A symbol of The Light of the World, the namesake of the season, the candles' historical significance was as a signal of welcome to travelers. The area itself attracts countless visitors each year, but one inn, the Williamsburg Inn, remains a destination in its own right. It's been a luxurious stay for celebrities, dignitaries, and guests from all over the world since it first opened its doors in 1937. During the holidays, three perfectly brilliant Christmas trees glow during the evenings to graciously welcome arriving guests, who are able to live like royalty—if only for a while.

GOVERNOR'S PALACE

The Governor's Palace at Williamsburg, Virginia, was home
to seven royal governors, Patrick Henry, and Thomas Jefferson.
Customarily, the presiding Governor hosted a ball during the 12
days of Christmas. On the highest occasions, lights might be put
in the windows of the little tower or lantern (or "lanthorn"
as it was called) that crowned the flat, balustraded roof.

The Jefferson Hotel
Richmond, Virginia

If you're dreaming of a white Christmas in the South, you may want to travel to Monkton, Maryland, to view the Ladew Topiary Gardens. In these gardens, created in 1937 by Harvey Smith Ladew, snow renders the ultimate transformative blessing. Within a night, it etches twig and berry, cottons shrub and lawn, and swallows every sound into the hush of a midwinter's dream.

Born into wealth and leisure, Ladew fancied everything English, especially the life of a country gentleman. He loved ladies, fine drink, horses, the hunt, and the hounds. Oh, and he loved country gardens, too. He'd never particularly cared about topiary, however, until one morning, while fox-hunting in England, he chanced upon a topiary portraying a fox hotly pursued by hounds. Smitten by the find, he reproduced it in his own landscape. Today, the hunt scene remains the garden's most iconic and photographed feature. The gardens quickly became a sensation when Ladew opened them to the public in 1971. Few Southerners had ever seen topiary on this grand a scale.

Heading south from Maryland into North Carolina, you, the holiday traveler, may happen upon another grand-scale destination nestled in the Blue Ridge Mountains in Asheville. Biltmore House, a 250-room French Renaissance château built by George Vanderbilt in the late 19th century, contains more than 4 acres of floor space and was the largest undertaking in residential architecture when construction began in 1889.

Biltmore dazzles with embellishments, transforming the magnificent estate into a winter wonderland. Bells, bows, and bangles perch on every pedestal, tabletop, and horizontal surface in the château. You could stand in one spot in any room, turn slowly for 15 minutes, and still feel as if you've missed something. You probably did.

Ladew Topiary Gardens
Monkton, Maryland

BILTMORE ESTATE, ASHEVILLE, NORTH CAROLINA

Biltmore Estate tops any holiday display south of the North Pole. As dusk settles, the glowing embers of sunset silhouette the towering building in soft orange and velvety purple. More than 300 luminarias flicker in subtle parchment hues, like so many Tinker Bells lining the huge panel of lawn.

ROOM FOR CELEBRATION

More than a hundred years ago, George Vanderbilt's dream house debuted with a fabulous
Christmas party. With 250 rooms, 4 acres of floors, and a dinner table that would seat 64,
making space for holiday guests at Biltmore Estate was no problem.

WOODLAND
RETREAT

If you're lucky enough to be in western North Carolina in the winter, do yourself a favor and cruise up and down the Blue Ridge Parkway. Sure, the scenery is magnificent any time of year, whether it is blanketed with spring blooms or ablaze in fall colors. But with less foliage and fewer travelers, the views of the rolling and wizened Blue Ridge Mountains and their complementing valleys seem to extend forever. As you wind along that famous road, you pass farms hemmed by wooden fences. They are pastoral scenes featuring horses and cattle that soothe your mind and stimulate your senses. This is cabin country, and with such a brisk climate at these elevations this time of year, it's no surprise to see the smoke from wood-burning fires curling up, up, up from chimneys. You can only imagine the cozy gatherings taking place around the hearths.

Tucked into a village just off the Blue Ridge Parkway, five generations of a Carolina family have savored hundreds of holiday meals, first in a small cottage and now in a home built using chestnut boards from the old house that go a long way toward capturing the heart of the original place. At Christmastime, the holiday table gleams with warm copper accents as the family gathers to celebrate another holiday season together.

HIGH-COUNTRY HOLIDAY

A new home replaces a family's early-1900s mountain cottage but maintains
the soul of the old house, which was taken down piece by piece—including windows,
stone, and wood—and is now ready for family gatherings for generations to come.

NATURAL INSPIRATION

Lovely and unique chestnut wood used throughout the house inspired the holiday trimmings
that draw from the abundance of fragrant native greenery in the woods surrounding the home.

A Wintry Yuletide Feast

You're invited to join us at the
fireside for a rustic repast.

Scarves and mittens suggested for
a walk in the woods at sunset.

A YULETIDE FEAST

Sweet Potato Soup

Arugula-Pear-Blue Cheese Salad

Cranberry Roasted Winter Vegetables

Pork Roast with Sweet Onion-
Pumpkin Seed Relish

Wild Rice with Bacon and Fennel

Gingerbread Soufflés

RECIPES ON PAGES 333-336

Arugula-Pear-Blue Cheese Salad

Sweet Potato Soup

PAIRS WELL WITH A CRACKLING FIRE

The sign of a successful dinner party isn't necessarily a scraped-clean plate. Rather, it's the unapologetic lingering that follows a satisfying meal—the warm, fuzzy, let's-stay-a-little-longer glow that stems from good conversation and good company. This menu is a delicious backdrop for just that.

Cranberry Roasted
Winter Vegetables

Pork Roast with Sweet Onion-
Pumpkin Seed Relish

Wild Rice with Bacon and Fennel

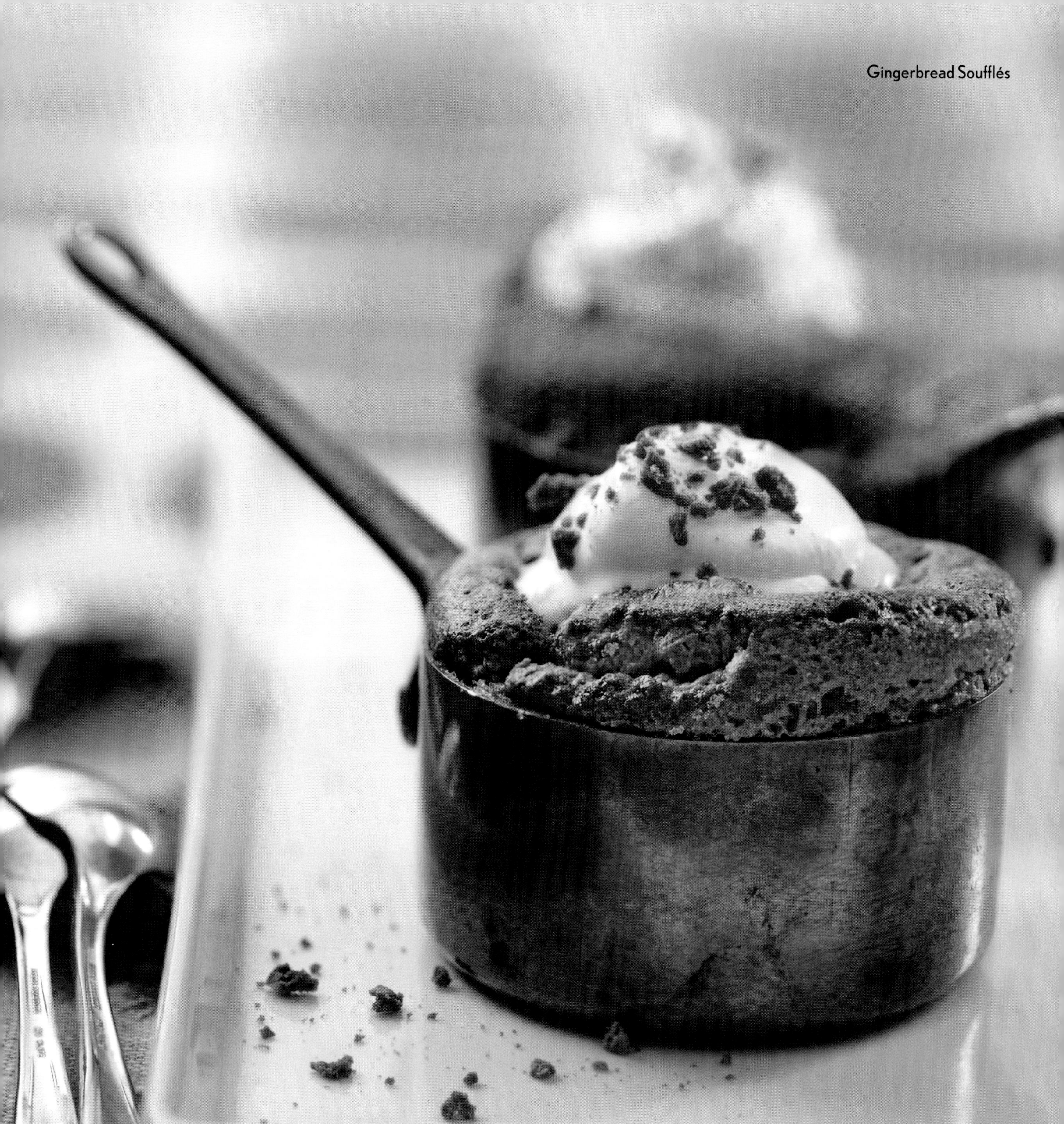

Gingerbread Soufflés

TO GRANDMOTHER'S HOUSE WE WENT

MARY ALLEN PERRY

My grandmother, Mamere, lived in a rambling old farmhouse she shared with Olivia, her longtime cook and traveling companion. It was a spacious house, but not at all grand by the standards of our fashionable relatives in the city. Its most remarkable feature was a long side porch that overlooked a pond where wild geese wintered. Mamere believed that porches were magical places, and that—like still waters and green pastures—they held the power to comfort and restore the soul.

On Christmas Eve, Olivia and Mamere would host a children's party and decorate the porch with miniature trees wrapped in garlands of sugarplums. Warmed with cocoa and quilts, we would nestle in the swing's calico cushions. There we would listen for the elusive sound of sleigh bells until we fell asleep, and our fathers would carry us home.

I inherited the role of Olivia's apprentice from a brother who abdicated the position after a Fourth of July fiasco involving a pitifully short strand of firecrackers attached to a wedge of watermelon. Our holiday Saturday afternoons were reserved for weekly marketing and five-and-dime sprees. Miss Edwina—an aging, ill-tempered spinster who was no relation, just Mamere's friend—thought we were absolutely reckless where money was concerned, though we preferred to think of ourselves as middle-of-the-road spendthrifts. According to Miss Edwina, there was no middle of the road. In fact, there was no road at all except the one to hell that Olivia and I were fast headed for if we didn't soon mend our ways.

Because Mamere's real passion was gardening, she rarely invaded Olivia's territory. Unfortunately, the same could not be said of Miss Edwina, who would arrive shortly after Halloween with a dead-tired disposition and a tiny box of coconut rum balls from Earline's Beauty Salon, where she had her seasonal cut and curl.

By the time Miss Edwina arrived, Mamere had already trimmed the house with candles and greenery, and the porch was filled with the smell of woodsmoke—an aroma signaling the advent of Olivia's holiday baking in the porch's wood-burning stove. It was a yearly ritual that began with a dozen batches of shortbread and culminated with a magnificent charlotte russe on Christmas Day.

The bounty and splendor of our holiday dinners were rivaled only by the food pavilion at the state fair. Our family would gather at my grandmother's house for an enormous midday meal. The ancient dining table, stretched to the limits of its arthritic frame, groaned beneath the weight of huge silver platters overflowing with roasted turkey and hickory-smoked ham. The ham was always glazed a bright mahogany red, with brown sugar and bourbon (a secret ingredient kept hidden beneath some loosened floorboards in the kitchen closet).

Crystal bowls brimming with fresh pickled peaches, spicy piccalilli, and candied cucumber chips lined the sideboard next to bundles of slender pole beans and pyramids of fried green tomatoes harvested before a late November frost.

There were baked apples, mounds of cornbread dressing with slivers of onion and sage, and tender young greens that had simmered for hours in cast-iron kettles. There were mashed potatoes and sweet potatoes and more desserts than a body could imagine. It all made for a series of glorious feasts with as many relatives and stories as there were recipes.

Over the years, our family has grown. The bounty and splendor of our holiday dinners is now often governed by our hectic work schedules and the distance between the cities that separate us—though we are all certain to have Olivia's ham and Mamere's asparagus casserole. And always, there are the stories that tell of eccentric relatives and old farmhouses and clear, cold nights on the edge of winter, when small children fell asleep in a porch swing, listening to the sound of sleigh bells, very distant and far away. ✘

HELEN, GEORGIA

Nestled in the Appalachians sits this little town that reinvented itself in 1969, when locals spearheaded a movement
to replace storefronts with facades inspired by Bavarian towns in the mountains of Germany. Today, Helen's
identity revolves around that German flavor, especially at Christmas, when the lights and decorations are on display.

RADIANT WONDERS

Onward to Callaway Gardens, where the staff does Christmas 365 days a year. It takes that much preparation work and focus to manage the 8 million lights (that's 731 miles of strands) and more than a dozen scenes set to music during the annual Fantasy In Lights, the biggest event anywhere near Pine Mountain, Georgia, from the middle of November until the end of the year. One of the ways the staff keeps the displays up to date is by frequently communicating with the Bill Ferrell Co., the California-based outfit that helped originally design Fantasy In Lights its first season more than 20 years ago. The West Coast company knows how to put on a show. It handles the lighting and sound for the Academy Awards and drops the confetti in Times Square at New Year's.

The best way to enjoy this magical trip through the paths and forests of one of the most famous gardens in the South is to book a ride on one of the festival's Jolly Trolleys. Sure, you can slowly idle your car through the more than 5 miles of trails. But it's better to let someone else while you marvel at the dazzling spectacle.

DREAMS AVENUE

Virginia Hand Callaway was the first to dream of a Christmas lights show at the Pine Mountain, Georgia, retreat that she co-founded with her husband. She fondly remembered from her childhood the Christmas light displays she enjoyed on lawns in her hometown. Her vision gradually took shape over the years, and in 1992 the switch was flipped on for the holiday light show at Callaway Gardens.

FANTASY IN LIGHTS

Almost as fantastic as the light show at Callaway is the fact that it takes two workers
at least 45 minutes every night to flip more than 1,000 switches to "turn on" the show
and another 45 minutes to turn it off at the end of the night.

Traveling east from the mountains of Georgia to the South Carolina Lowcountry, you'll find one of the belles of Southern cities. Charleston remains one of the most fabulous and memorable destinations in the entire South, no matter the season. This time of year, however, the city—with its architectural marvels, towering church spires, green spaces, waterfront walks, Spanish moss-covered live oaks, and historic neighborhoods—particularly sparkles.

The lights lining the cables of the two diamond-shaped towers that define the Ravenel Bridge become doubly impressive in the evenings when seen reflecting in the Cooper River below. More lights stretch up the 60-foot-tall Christmas tree (you can walk beneath it!) in Marion Square, one of the city's most popular parks. Still more twinkling lights drape the state's iconic palmetto trees found throughout this jewel of the Lowcountry.

If you'd like a taste of what Charleston was like 250 years ago, book a room at the John Rutledge House Inn. Built in 1763 for John Rutledge, one of the signers of the U.S. Constitution, the 19-room inn is filled with antiques and historically accurate reproductions to give the feel of an old Charleston home. At breakfast, the staff serves local specialties such as shrimp and grits with biscuits and sherried fruit in the Signers Ballroom where, it's said, parts of the Constitution were drafted.

ELEGANTLY FESTIVE

This South Carolina city's charm and grace abound year-round, but at Christmastime it's especially enchanting. The multifaceted allure of the area features seasonal highlights such as a 3-mile Festival of Lights nighttime driving tour, season-long festivities at Marion Square that include the lighting of the Charleston Christmas Tree, and an annual Holiday Progressive Dinner with stops at popular restaurants for hors d'oeuvres, dinner, and, to end the evening, coffee and desserts at historic John Rutledge House Inn.

Historic Charleston

Ravenel Bridge

Marion Square

John Rutledge House Inn

LOWCOUNTRY LIFESTYLE

South of Charleston flows the Beaufort River where glowing, string light-lined vessels slowly ease their way during Beaufort's Light Up the Town boat parade. This processional speaks to the sweet, simple way of life enjoyed by the locals who call this region of the South home. Even in this modern age, an imaginative mind has the ability to transport a person back—way back—to a time in the 16th century when Spanish settlers first discovered this coastal paradise. The saltwater marshes, low-hanging live oak trees, and pure beauty surely drew them to this place then and continue to now.

The uniqueness of this place carries over to the houses and cottages detailed with clapboard siding and tin roofs and set back from the banks of the Intracoastal Waterway. At the holidays, many remain modest in their decorating—again, a nod to the simple way of life—drawing from a repertoire of garlands and silver.

You find it in the Christmas Parade, some 100 or so units comprising floats, marching bands, and the occasional fancy car. You can hear it in the voices of the Parris Island Marine Corps band as they perform during the annual A Night on the Town, when downtown streets become pedestrian-friendly, shops stay open long into the evening, and Santa arrives to help light the city's Christmas tree.

People have long known and celebrated this jewel among the barrier islands of South Carolina. And if you have never met Beaufort, this would be the perfect time of year to initiate an introduction.

CLASSIC CAROLINA CHRISTMAS

Framed by trees fittingly adorned for the holidays with Spanish moss, a traditional
Lowcountry cottage dressed with simple yet sophisticated flourishes awaits holiday guests.

COOKIES, COCKTAILS & CAROLS

༄

Let's enjoy festive sips
and sweets as we sing our way
into the holiday spirit!

COOKIES & COCKTAILS

Gingerbread Linzer Cookies

Spiced Sorghum Snowflakes

Almond Poinsettia Cookies

Coconut Snowballs

Sparkling Cranberry Cider

Chocolate Cream Martini

Caramel Apple Cider

RECIPES ON PAGES 337-340

Sparkling
Cranberry Cider

Gingerbread Linzer Cookies,
Spiced Sorghum Snowflakes,
Coconut Snowballs, Sparkling
Cranberry Cider

Chocolate Cream Martini

Almond Poinsettia Cookies

COZY AND SWEET

'Tis the season to use a colorful array of sugars, sprinkles, luster dust, and more
to dress fanciful treats in seasonal style.

Caramel Apple Cider,
Almond Poinsettia Cookies,
Spiced Sorghum Snowflakes

SIEGFRIED AND JOY

ALLISON GLOCK

Last Christmas, my husband (known here as Mr. Beasley) and I decided to experiment with a nontraditional holiday. For as long as I can remember, I have been, let's say, thematically inclined. I've never met a vintage decoration I didn't like. I harvest natural boughs for garland. I string twinkle lights from every doorjamb. I bow-up the dogs. Then I bake. And make treat baskets for my friends and neighbors. With hand-embroidered napkins inside. Featuring holiday motifs.

It is a sickness. One that afflicts my entire family of origin. Maybe because we lived so many years in one-season Florida, we felt the need to overcompensate. Every year, my mother would unpack the multitudes of cardboard boxes crammed with ornaments, velveteen red ribbons, and snow-sprayed pinecone wreaths. No shelf escaped an elf or porcelain Santa. If Christmas had a pride parade, it would look like our house.

Problem is, playing hillbilly Martha Stewart is time-consuming and expensive. It also, according to Mr. Beasley, can make a person grumpy.

"Next year let's just go away someplace instead," my husband suggested after weathering a particularly grueling season wherein I had enlisted his help with the napkin sewing and made him watch the entire *Gilmore Girls* box set.

"Who would water the tree?" I asked.

"We wouldn't have a tree," he said with unconcealed enthusiasm. One look into his squinty sewing eyes and I knew he wasn't kidding. "Some people actually relax on their holidays," he added stiffly.

A deal was struck. In two years, he could design the Christmas vacation. Which is how last Noel we ended up in Vegas with 20 members of Mr. Beasley's extended family.

Initially, I was lost. With no seasonal chores to do, I found myself idle for the first time in decades. Instead of cooking and decorating, I went zip-lining with the kids. In lieu of art-directing our tree, we posed for snapshots in front of the casino's 22-footer adorned with stuffed tigers. There was no caroling, but there was David Copperfield, and a roller coaster, and all we could eat.

Susan, Mr. Beasley's statuesque, red-headed aunt from Amarillo, sensed my unease. A schoolteacher for 30 years, she likened my displacement to the way she felt during the summer months. "It's hard for Southern women to do nothing," she said sagely. "We like to feel useful. It's how we show we care."

And there it was in a chestnut-shell. My Christmas obsession wasn't about the holiday at all. It was about creating a space that felt like love. A magical, light-filled fantasy reflecting promise and hope and dreams we pray will come true. Not so far off from Vegas, actually. Only with fewer drunk Santas. And a lot more sugar. 🖎

Heartfelt Gatherings

HEARTFELT
GATHERINGS

We have finally arrived. Christmas!
Some of us have been building to this point all year
long—have viewed the 364 days preceding this one
as merely a prologue to what has been called the "sudden new joy"
that wells up inside of us until we are engulfed in an enthusiasm
matched only by the most significant life points, such as a wedding
day or the birth of a child.

This is why we worked so hard to forage and prune and hang every piece of garland. To dog-ear every relevant magazine story featuring the latest and greatest decorating tips (who knew you could do that with a galvanized bucket?). To tear out every scrumptious-sounding recipe—the ridged edges reminding us of classic yellowed clippings our mothers and grandmothers kept stacked amidst the pages of their favorite cookbooks. To reserve the best table at the best restaurant weeks in advance for the most delicious holiday feast. To take that one last walk around the tree to make sure that it stands arrow-straight and that we have trimmed it just right with all the lights sparkling in the perfect places.

This is the pinnacle of excitement for the whole season. The Christmas season is all about coming home, about the people we love and cherish. And by this time, all the friends and family members, who might come home just one time per year, have survived the flights and rides and drives just to get here.

Sometimes they slide in at the last minute a bit harried and ruffled, their shoulders overburdened with bags. They've carried the trip with them, but they leave it just outside the doorstep. Because when they walk over that threshold and finally stop to embrace the familiar—the very embodiment of home—all those memories rush back and instantly alleviate all holiday travel stress.

The reconnection begins. It could happen with each person taking turns sharing an update. Or, more subtly, the news from each family member slowly reveals itself over a board game. Or maybe the family just gathers to watch their favorite Christmas movie—the one they see every year, the one where they whisper the lines along with the actors, the one that triggers the emotions of happy memories with scenes such as Scrooge in his post-ghost euphoria joyously trotting down Main Street in *A Christmas Carol;* the ringing bell signifying Clarence finally receiving his wings in *It's a Wonderful Life;* Ralphie's exuberance at finally being able to aim his Red Ryder BB gun in *A Christmas Story;* or Clark Griswold, with his wide grin, beholding his magnificently gaudy work of holiday light art in *Christmas Vacation.*

No matter the tradition, everyone is present. Everyone is in the moment.

Southall Eden
Lepiers Fork, Tennessee

In *One Writer's Beginnings*, Southern writer Eudora Welty talks about the subtle nature of her father's intentional gifts to instill his children with his own belief that exciting and innovative prospects always lie ahead.

From our earliest Christmas times, Santa Claus brought us toys that instruct boys and girls (separately) how to build things—stone blocks cut to the castle-building style, Tinker Toys, and Erector sets. Daddy made for us himself elaborate kites that needed to be taken miles out of town to a pasture long enough (and my father was not afraid of horses and cows watching) for him to run with and get up on a long cord to which my mother held the spindle, and then we children were given it to hold, tugging like something alive at our hands. They were beautiful, sound, shapely box kites, smelling delicately of office glue for their entire short lives. And of course as soon as the boys attained anywhere near the right age, there was an electric train, the engine with its pea-sized working headlight, its line of cars, tracks equipped with switches, semaphores, its station, its bridges, and its tunnel, which blocked off all other traffic in the upstairs hall. Even from downstairs, and through the cries of excited children, the elegant rush and click of the train could be heard through the ceiling, running around and around its figure eight.

All of this, but especially the train, represents my father's fondest beliefs—in progress, in the future. With these gifts, he was preparing his children.

Despite all of the rushing around—the shopping, the baking, the partying—this time of year also lends itself to healthy, calming, and thoughtful introspection. It is a time to delicately balance the memories of the past with the moments of the present and the visions of the future. It is a time to exhale and tune in to yourself. To remember all of your holidays leading to this one and the meaningful people who populate those memories. To account for your place in this world, in this life. And to dream about your next steps and where your path might lead.

Your home now becomes the heart of the holidays, and the family table centers the merrymaking. We now usher you into a celebration of Christmas Eve and Christmas Day traditions.

Three Chimneys Farm
Midway, Kentucky

O CRACKER BARREL

ACE ATKINS

I have a confession. I really like Cracker Barrel. Never mind that its rocking chair-crowded front porch is perched on the edge of an interstate. Beneath all those washer boards and John Deere mugs is a landmark of my childhood.

On the long drive home for the holidays, a Cracker Barrel signaled that we had crossed the Mason-Dixon Line back into God's Country. Our family hailed from Alabama but lived for a while in Detroit and St. Louis, where Dad was an NFL coach. We'd drive home on Christmas Eve or December 26, and Cracker Barrel was the only thing open. It was usually one of the first stops on the trip. My old man drove the route with the intensity of Jerry Reed in *Smokey and the Bandit* and once famously passed me a Coke bottle rather than stop for a restroom. Because we usually started to travel at night, by dawn I would watch for the billboards with the brown-and-yellow logo—32 miles, 17 miles, 5 miles . . . the wait seemed to last forever.

A 10-year-old does not distinguish real from authentic, or roll their eyes at the corny old ads of Ty Cobb selling tobacco, or even notice the sweatshirts spelling World's Greatest Grandma in floral appliqué. I just could not wait to get real country ham and biscuits. (In Detroit, salty country ham did not exist. My grandmother Leila would occasionally mail it to me from the Winn-Dixie along with a can of boiled peanuts.)

At the restaurant, my mom used the pay phone to call her folks to let them know our progress. I was allotted one toy. Most often it was fake dog poop, a whoopee cushion, or a corncob pipe—anything that would make my grandfather laugh or annoy my sister. We waited for our breakfast while playing that infamous golf-tee board game where leaving four or more tees meant you were an eg-no-ra-moose.

The restaurant always had holiday music playing and a great-smelling fire going in a huge rock fireplace, usually with a Christmas tree nearby. My family would gather 'round the fire and eat our holiday biscuits, not caring if the fire and the biscuits were franchised up and down the South's interstates. For us, it meant we were almost home.

MERRY

AND

BRIGHT

There is a palpable buzz in the air no soul can deny. For children, the family Christmas Eve dinner may just as well be a penance, another obstacle that must be hurdled, a wide and deep chasm that must be crossed to reach Christmas morning. Those pint-sized bundles of pure anticipation are more keyed up and wound more tightly than at any other point in the year.

Who can eat at a time like this? A jolly man with copious amounts of toys is about to descend on our house! And here we politely and quietly sit at the table. Oh, the questions. Did all my messages throughout the year make it to Santa? Will he hold my naughtiness against me? Did he notice my extra effort to be particularly nice, especially in these past few weeks? But that buzz extends to the adults as well, right? Frankly, they constitute their own anticipatory packages and are also more keyed up and tightly wound than at any other time of year. Oh, their questions. Did "Santa" remember that the bike was supposed to be blue? Wait, was it supposed to be blue? And, despite the color, does "Santa" have enough time and skill to assemble said bike?

With these dual perspectives in the mix, what this ultimately means is that Christmas Eve dinner often occupies a tone that skews toward the informal. Decorative items, and even the recipes themselves, embody a more playful character. Conversations are lively, but most of the younger guests at the table probably fall prey to distraction because they have all cocked at least one ear toward the ceiling to listen for hoof steps.

The bottom line is that Santa is on his way. Neither a buffet spread nor high water will stop him.

ABUNDANCE OF SWEETNESS

There are no rules on Christmas Eve, right? That makes it the perfect occasion to splurge—whether it's to indulge with a candy buffet (that makes a pretty cute decoration, by the way) or to simply sit back and share the magic and wonder of the day with family and friends.

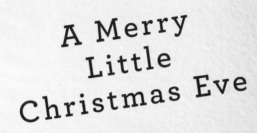

A Merry Little Christmas Eve

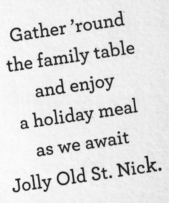

Gather 'round
the family table
and enjoy
a holiday meal
as we await
Jolly Old St. Nick.

A MERRY CHRISTMAS EVE DINNER

Classic Eggnog

Honey-Rosemary Cherries
and Blue Cheese Crostini

Spice-Rubbed Smoked Turkey Breast
with Mushroom Gravy

Pecan Cornbread

Butternut Squash Casserole
with Pecan Streusel

Crumb-Topped Spinach Casserole

Cranberry Clementine Relish

White Chocolate-Peppermint
Mousse Pie

RECIPES ON PAGES 341-345

Honey-Rosemary Cherries
and Blue Cheese Crostini

Spice-Rubbed Smoked
Turkey Breast
with Mushroom Gravy

Crumb-Topped Spinach
Casserole

AND TO ALL A GOOD MEAL

The Christmas Eve supper may play second fiddle to the following day's grand meal, but this menu,
with its delectable mix of sweet and savory dishes, is a fine way to start the celebration.

White Chocolate-Peppermint Mousse Pie

O HOLY NIGHT

In the midst of all the bright lights and sounds of Christmas, this is the one sure solace. While Christmas Eve dinner probably charged the air, the Christmas Eve service possesses the power to slow, and sometimes even halt, the frenetic pace of the season.

The details are so simple, yet completely effective. Like waves flapping a shoreline, the randomly ordered flickers from candles induce calm and serene spirits. Christmas hymns and songs, those permanent tones in the rhythm of our lives, allow us to recalibrate ourselves. And though the message likely never strays too far from the previous year's or the one before that, we admittedly cannot be reminded enough that this season represents more than the bright lights and the sounds outside.

Because inside we observe a reverence that cradles us. Inside we are gifted with time to reflect on our own lives and what we have. Inside we are surrounded by our tangible blessings, the people who share kindred beliefs, the people who support us, the people who share our bloodline and history, the people we love.

ALL SAINTS' CHAPEL
SEWANEE, TENNESSEE

For more than 50 years, in early December, an annual Festival of Lessons and Carols has been held at the elegantly serene All Saints' Chapel, which stands at the center of Sewanee's campus.

All Saints' Chapel, Sewanee, Tennessee

Crescent Hill Baptist Church
Helen, Georgia

"For me Christmas is a celebration of the birth of Christ. I never let my family forget that."

—JIMMY CARTER

EVERY ONE INTO HIS OWN CITY

VALERIE FRASER LUESSE

And it came to pass in those days . . .
I read those words and am immediately transported back home, back to a small Baptist church where the annual Christmas program helped us say goodbye to the year past, prepare for a new one to come, and celebrate the faith that bound us together from one winter to the next.

Growing up, I never felt like winter had truly arrived until I had practiced my part in the program at least once or twice. Blame it on Alabama, where September might as well be a summer month, and even October has trouble making up its mind to get cold. Only in late November, when choir rehearsals began in earnest, could we pretty much count on frosty mornings and cold, clear nights.

It's worth noting that my home church had Christmas programs, not pageants. For us, the word "pageant" lacked a certain dignity. It conjured images of Santa Claus and beauty queens. A program, on the other hand, was a solemn affair, requiring song cues and solos and difficult music. And it also should be noted that over the years our little church presented some truly fine programs. We even surprised ourselves with the beautiful music we were able to share with our community. Still, it is the momentary lapses, those unpredictable imperfections, that I remember most fondly.

Once, when I was about 7, my cousin Kathy and I had to portray angels (as in "Hark! The Herald . . ."). Our mothers made our robes of white bedsheets, cut our wings out of poster board, and glued silver garland around their edges. Halos made of garland-wrapped coat hangers completed our celestial ensembles. Thus bedecked, Kathy and I stood on either side of the pulpit, our arms stretched heavenward, while the choir sang every single one of the verses of that carol. Twenty-eight years have passed, and my arms still cramp when I hear that song.

Then, of course, there was the elusive Star in the East, beamed onto the church wall with a slide projector. One year it failed to appear where the wise man expected. Undaunted, he just kept pointing and pivoting, repeating his well-rehearsed line—"Follow the Star!"—until at last his finger was aimed at the right wall.

By the time I became a teenager, we had begun hiring part-time choir directors from Birmingham. All of them were studying music at one university or another, and most were either married or engaged to a soprano who could really hit the high notes. They liked to do cantatas, 40-page musical extravaganzas with Christmas songs that nobody in Shelby County, Alabama, had ever heard. They assured us that the congregation would receive a blessing, and, as an afterthought, they casually mentioned that if we locked our knees during the lengthy performance, we could easily pass out right there in the choir loft.

As the Christmas program drew nearer, the entire choir would move, in emotional unison, from mild apprehension to out-and-out panic. "We still aren't coming in together! We've never sung the whole thing all the way through!"

In the end, most of us generally did miss a note or two. And something usually did go wrong with the lights or the microphones or other technical stuff. But it never mattered. When the last note was sung and we heard those amens coming from the congregation, all we could feel was an overwhelming flood of joy, relief, and prayerful thanks for the bonds that have held our community together for generations, winter to winter. 🖋

LAISSEZ LES BON TEMPS ROULER

Réveillon dinners are a Christmas Eve tradition in French-speaking regions across the globe. These festive parties feature elaborate, luxurious, multicourse feasts that can extend into the early morning hours. (Réveillon is French for "awakening," and on Christmas Eve, the dinners customarily began after Catholic families participated in Mass.)

In the South, Louisiana families—with their rich, ever-present Creole heritage—have privately celebrated this holiday tradition as long as anyone can remember.

In the 1990s, however, the city of New Orleans decided to bring Réveillon dinners to the public, tourists, and other visitors who had come to town to experience the seasonal delights of the Big Easy. Restaurants were encouraged to host nightly feasts throughout the month of December with menus inspired by the tradition's staple foods—egg dishes, puddings, breads, soups, seafood, and veal. Today, many of the classic and rising restaurants alike feature Réveillon dinners, a prix fixe menu of three, four, five, or more courses—turtle soup, oyster chowder, gumbo, shrimp rémoulade, crab ravioli, English toffee bread, and pecan bread pudding, among other decadent delicacies.

ARNAUD'S, NEW ORLEANS, LOUISIANA

Diners don dinner jackets and cocktail dresses and linger at tables with friends and family for hours while jazz trios play on and on and on, improvising and swaying until dawn.

CRESCENT CITY STYLE

In New Orleans, traditions are as thick as roux, and the fetes start early with a month of Réveillon dinners.
Celebrations culminate with towering bonfires ablaze on the levees, lighting up the bayou.

FEUX DE JOIE

Late in the evening, just before Christmas Day, a casual observer will spot bright sparks originating from popping sugarcane reeds sailing through the night like shooting stars. Known as feux de joie (fires of joy), the bonfires on the Mississippi River levees around Louisiana (including New Orleans, the small town of Lutcher in St. James Parish, and others) are believed to light the way to midnight Mass, or guide Papa Noel and his gator-pulled boat through dark swamps to the homes of Cajun children. Cold hands pass hot gumbo and jambalaya late into the night, when the shouts become murmurs and towering blazes subside to glowing embers.

OUR TRAVELING CHRISTMAS

MARK CHILDRESS

When I was little, we lived in Ohio and Indiana, but my extremely Southern parents made sure we never spent a Christmas there. Let Bing Crosby sing about sleigh bells in the snow. To our family, Christmas meant a journey from a snowy clime to the warmer latitudes of the Deep South. For weeks, my brothers and I would study the growing pile of packages in the living room. Then one cold afternoon Daddy would load the car—without warning, so we wouldn't drive him crazy beforehand. Only a man who loved packing could have artfully jammed all that stuff, three wild boys, and our mom into one Oldsmobile, but even with his skill there was always an overflow tied to the roof.

Daddy always timed our departure for late in the day, the idea being that somewhere between Louisville and Nashville we youngsters would fidget ourselves to sleep. But the excitement of Christmas and the sensation of frigid Midwest December air giving way to warmer Southern breezes tended to keep us awake.

The idea of transporting our whole Christmas 600 miles in a car worked out well, with two notable exceptions. One year my brother Rory's present for Mom was a bottle of fancy shampoo with a screw-off doll's head for a cap. (Trust me. It was sweet.) Somehow the doll's head came off, and shampoo seeped over all our presents and clothes. Christmas that year was imbued with a soapy lavender aroma.

Another year Daddy's arrangement of packages on the roof proved a shade less artful than usual. Our entire Christmas slid off along a half-mile stretch of interstate highway. We had the unforgettable experience of running up and down the shoulder of the highway, dodging traffic as we gathered up broken toys and splayed-open suitcases.

Our arrival at Granny's house was a middle-of-the-night event, a sleepy memory of being carried from the car to soft white sheets. We were lucky enough to have two grandmothers barely 100 miles apart, a terribly fortuitous circumstance when you're a kid and Christmas is involved. We would start the celebration with one tree and a pile of presents at Granny's house, and when that pile (and Granny) became exhausted, we'd move on to Grandmother's house in Butler County. That was where Santa Claus really found us. Oh, yes, Santa Claus was real. Sure, he had help from our parents and grandparents and our Aunt Hanna, but we remained certain of his existence—and omnipotence.

Long before dawn, we'd wake up, and then it was a matter of waiting for 5 a.m.—or whatever time our parents had decreed as the absolute minimum earliest. At last we'd creep out from under the covers into the icy room and pull on the flannel bathrobes and slippers we never wore any other morning of the year. It's impossible to describe the joy we took from those mornings: all those presents. Our family wrapped their gifts in fancy paper, but Santa Claus simply left big piles of wonderful loot arrayed in three corners of the room, one for each boy.

The rest of the day was a marvelous blur—a groaning dinner table, laughter, and touch football in the yard. It was a time for lap-sitting, fire-gazing, storytelling. Happiness came easily to everyone. Nobody cried on Christmas.

Then Grandmother died, at Christmastime, and everybody cried.

Now when I hear Bing Crosby singing about Christmas, I think of Grandmother and those years, that place, three excited little boys with teeth chattering from the first chill of the parlor. I remember the time I discovered a secret I really did not want to know. In the years since, though, I have managed to unlearn that secret. Once again I believe that Santa Claus is alive and well—and living in the South. ✽

CHRISTMAS
DAY

Yes, you've all been awake since daybreak—possibly even before then—swept up in the giddy reveal of gift ("Wow!") after gift ("Yes!") after gift ("Awesome!"). Every ounce of bridled anticipation has finally been released, and everyone's giant smiles are only occasionally interrupted by late-morning yawns.

Parker S.

PANCAKES
&
PRESENTS

❄

Let's begin the big day opening gifts
and enjoying a jolly
Christmas morning brunch!

CHRISTMAS MORNING BRUNCH

Winter Citrus Mocktail

Cinnamon Coffee with
Bourbon Cream

Hummingbird Pancakes

Italian Cream Pancakes

Carrot Cake Pancakes

Red Velvet Pancakes

German Chocolate Pancakes

Caramel Cake Pancakes

RECIPES ON PAGES 346-351

Carrot Cake Pancakes

Caramel Cake Pancakes

German Chocolate Pancakes

Red Velvet Pancakes

Hummingbird Pancakes   Italian Cream Pancakes

MAGICAL MORNING

Recipes for this Christmas morning pancake extravaganza were all adapted
from classic Southern cake recipes.

THE GIFT OF WRAPPING

BETH ANN FENNELLY

One of my earliest, happiest Christmas memories concerns a box wrapped in a Victorian teddy bear paper. I was 6 and had to have a Madame Alexander doll. On Christmas morning, I opened the teddy bears to find my much desired companion. While I hugged her, my thrifty mother smoothed the wrapping and laid it aside.

When it turned up under the tree the next December, it was like spotting an old friend. Thereafter, the teddy bears always adorned a favorite gift. Every year, the paper shrank as it was torn and trimmed. Eventually, it might stretch to cover a book, or, later still, earrings. Nowadays the remnant is the size of a matchbook, but still Mom affixes it to a larger piece to wrap something special.

I, too, have a paper for each of my three children that—through clever origami, strategic name tags, and double-sided tape—covers a favorite gift. Come December, you'll find me stretching it like an artist stretching a canvas, then creating my humble art, tucking hospital corners around the boxes, squealing scissors down the curling ribbon. After placing my best-dressed presents under our lit tree, I brush pine needles from my shoulders and stand back to admire the patchwork of Christmases past and future.

The home-wrapped gift has gone the way of the handwritten thank-you, I'm afraid.

It saves time to have presents store-wrapped or popped in one-size-fits-all bags with puffs of tissue. But I'll have to cut corners elsewhere. For me, wrapping is not only a meaningful flourish—it is also my deeply centering preparation. Wrapping must be done in secrecy, so in those busy weeks of shopping and parties, those hours are the only ones I spend alone. And when wrapping gifts, I'm thinking about their recipients—how creative my son is with his Legos, how gracefully my ill friend has struggled, how much I owe my mother. It seasons me for the season. I don't wrap gifts for others, not really. Wrapping gifts is the gift I give myself.

A TIME TO SHINE

If any meal stamps the exclamation point on this big day, it is the Christmas Dinner. This is the time in the season to produce all your elegant decor and the accoutrements to complement your grandiose spread. Plates supported by chargers. Elaborate bouquets spilling from their vases. Fine linen napkins, displayed like individual pieces of art, folded beside place cards featuring calligraphy.

FRIENDSHIPS AND FAMILY TIES

The peaceful pace that descends the week after Christmas affords us the luxury of focusing
on all the things most important to us that, in other times of the year, have receded into our minds. We have not
forgotten them, but it is the Christmas Dinner that elevates them to the surface and initiates our reverie.

A Joyful Christmas Dinner

Please join us for
a festive dinner party.

Come over early
for cocktails
& merry mingling.

CHRISTMAS DINNER

Ruby Red Negroni

Pecan Soup

Honey-Curry Glazed Lamb with
Roasted Grapes and Cranberries

Green Beans with Hollandaise Sauce

Savory Bacon-and-Leek
Bread Pudding

Roasted Beets with Herbed
Dijon Vinaigrette

Gingersnap-Meyer Lemon
Meringue Tart

RECIPES ON PAGES 352-355

Honey-Curry Glazed Lamb with
Roasted Grapes and Cranberries,
Roasted Beets with Herbed Dijon
Vinaigrette, Savory Bacon-and-
Leek Bread Pudding, Green Beans
with Hollandaise Sauce

Ruby Red Negroni

Honey-Curry Glazed Lamb with
Roasted Grapes and Cranberries

GRAND AND GRACIOUS

The day's repast begins with a storied aperitif, the Negroni, and culminates
with an almost-too-beautiful-to-eat tart—what more could you expect for such a special day?

Gingersnap-Meyer Lemon Meringue Tart

THE
GRAND
FINALE

The white cake was traditionally served on the Twelfth Night of Christmas to celebrate the Epiphany. Today, it is enjoyed on any festive night. Underneath that white frosting lie flavors limited only by your imagination. It may be coconut lemon or chocolate truffle, red-velvet-peppermint or pecan divinity.

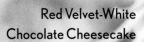

Holiday Cakes

Indulge in a wonderland
of fantastic frosted
confections.

CHRISTMAS CAKES

Chocolate-Toffee-Gingerbread Cake

Bourbon Eggnog Cake

Red Velvet Cake with Coconut-Cream Cheese Frosting

Tiramisù Layer Cake

SLICE OF HOLIDAY GLEE

The enchanting white cake can be the glorious end to a celebratory meal, or it can be the featured star,
requiring only a cup of hot coffee in a supporting role. Either way, these cakes are winners in any category.

Snowy White Layer Cake

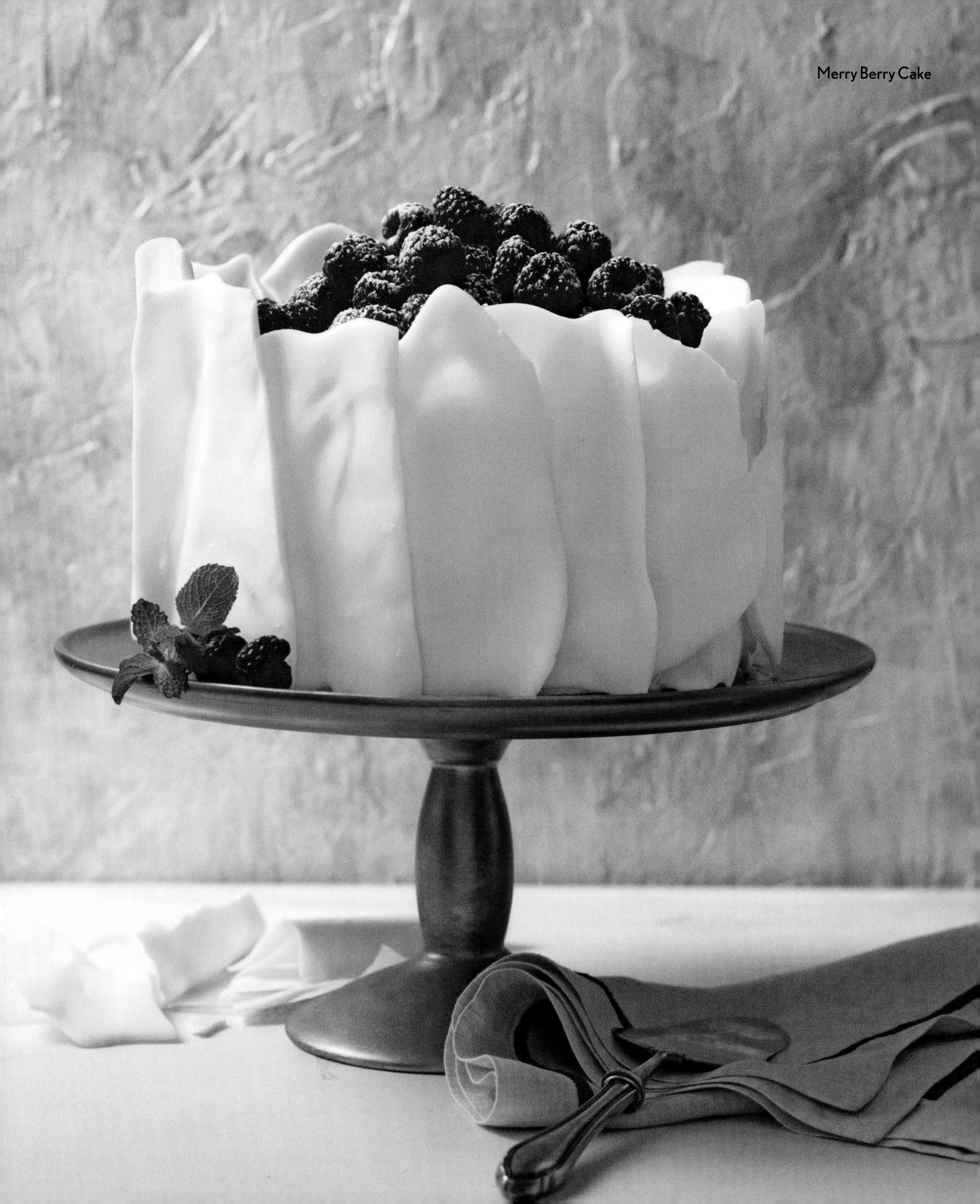
Merry Berry Cake

Layered Peppermint Cheesecake

Marbled Pumpkin Praline Cake,
Peppermint-Hot Chocolate Cake

Gilded Bourbon-Chocolate Cake

I missed Christmas away from home, I thought. What I really missed was a memory, an old memory of people long since gone, of my grandparents' house bursting with cousins, smilax, and holly. I missed the sound of hunting boots, the sudden open-door gusts of chilly air that cut through the aroma of pine needles and oyster dressing. I missed my brother's night-before-Christmas mask of rectitude and my father's bumblebee bass humming "Joy to the World."

—HARPER LEE, "Christmas to Me"

SPARKLING CELEBRATIONS

Our journey through these glorious holidays has finally reached its end. During those days between Christmas and New Year's, we have recharged ourselves, slowly edging our toes to the last step of the year. But before we pack it all up, sweep away the merriment, and enter the potential-filled New Year, we must pause one final time to celebrate all the remarkable experiences from the past 12 months.

A time to recharge your batteries. A time to prepare for that New Year when we make changes and better ourselves.

THE COUNTDOWN BEGINS

I f you aren't joining a celebration on New Year's Eve down here, it's not because you lack options. In Memphis, tens of thousands of people take to the streets for the Countdown on Beale, which includes a giant guitar dropped at midnight and the healthy practice called "burying your blues," in which you cast off some memento (everything from a traffic ticket to a photo from a fizzled relationship) that reminds you of an unhappy time during the year. Atlanta praises and drops its sacred peach at midnight, while the blessed city of New Orleans does the same with a lighted fleur de lis before blasting fireworks over the Mississippi River.

Perhaps you are noticing a theme. In our last act of the year, we Southerners get creative and hoist all manner of wild, weird, and wonderful things, just so we can tick them down.

Pensacola drops a 13- by 17-foot, half-ton lighted aluminum pelican sculpture. In Mobile, Alabama, a 12-foot-tall, 600-pound, electronic lighted chocolate MoonPie descends. The crowd in Havre de Grace, Maryland, blows on duck calls while watching a large duck decoy lowered from a fire truck ladder. Mt. Olive, North Carolina, has a pickle; Fredericksburg, Virginia, has a pear; and Ty Ty, Georgia, has a peanut. You'll find a live possum humanely lowered in a cage (then released back into the wild) at midnight in Brasstown, North Carolina. And you'll spy a stuffed possum lowered in a cage (then redisplayed at the Bud Jones Taxidermy Museum) in Tallapoosa, Georgia.

No matter where you are, this grand examination and exhalation is always best commemorated with a party. And no other place parties like we do in the South.

With the Blue Ridge Mountains as a backdrop, fireworks light the sky over the buzzing city of Asheville, North Carolina.

NEW YEAR REVELRIES

We have reached a meridian, a point that straddles the old year and the new. This is a time to celebrate the place we have attained and to mentally organize all that we have achieved, just so that we can fully appreciate it. This is also a time for a fresh restart, a time to slough off the burdens that weigh us, so that we can move forward into this new phase with the lightest steps possible.

Tomorrow, we will follow the Southern tradition of arming ourselves with collard greens and black-eyed peas, foods to ensure luck and prosperity. According to folklore, this auspicious New Year's Day custom dates back to the Civil War, when Union troops pillaged the land, leaving behind only black-eyed peas and greens as animal fodder. Rich in nutrients, these were the humble foods that enabled Southerners to survive. Some say the peas represent coins and greens dollar bills that can even be tacked to the ceiling for good luck or hung over the door to ward off evil spirits. Even the pot likker, the juice left in a pot after collards cook, is traditionally valued as a delicacy and aphrodisiac.

Yes, in the morning, we will rise to a sunny winter's day and begin making our own luck, but tonight we lift sparklers to the sky to illuminate our faces and portend bright futures. Our chatter here at this evening's party is hopeful and realistic as we solidify the promises we make to our friends and our families to better ourselves. We raise our glasses in unison because before we can truly step into the New Year, we must tie a bow around the old. Let's party!

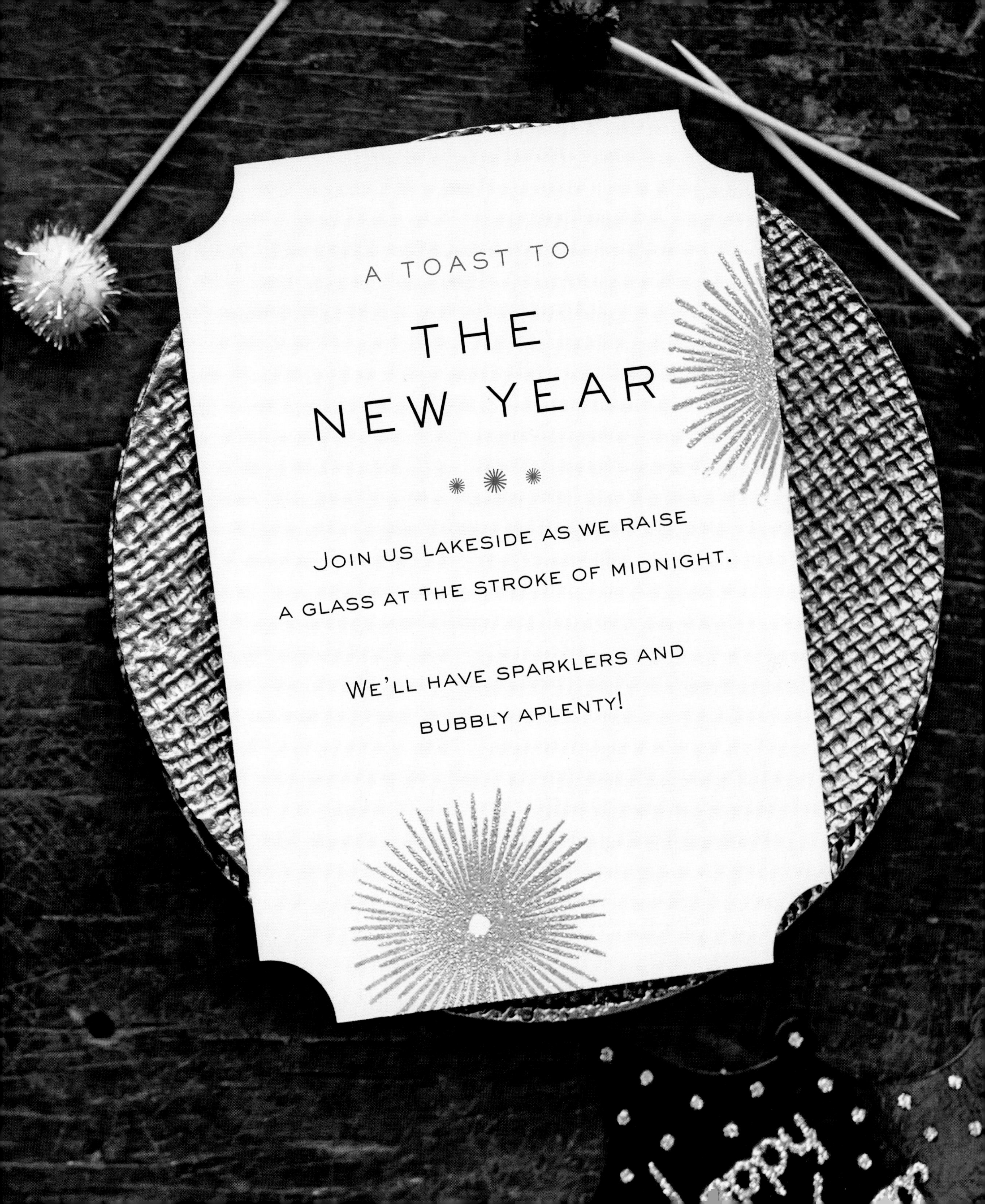

A TOAST TO

THE
NEW YEAR

* ** *

JOIN US LAKESIDE AS WE RAISE
A GLASS AT THE STROKE OF MIDNIGHT.

WE'LL HAVE SPARKLERS AND
BUBBLY APLENTY!

NEW YEAR'S EVE AT THE LAKE

Spiked Satsuma Champagne

Southern 75

Lemony Feta Dip
with Oven-Roasted Tomatoes

Bacon-Wrapped Bourbon Figs

Pickled Shrimp

Parmesan-Crusted Crab Cake Bites
with Chive Aïoli

Grits Crostini

Asparagus with Curry Dip

Raspberry Panna Cotta

German Chocolate Cake Truffles

Tiny Caramel Tarts

RECIPES ON PAGES 370-375

Lemony Feta Dip with
Oven-Roasted Tomatoes

GOOD LUCK AND GOOD CHEER

At this New Year's Eve party, we may be feasting on small bites—mobile munchies that encourage us to

circulate guest to guest—but we are toasting big ideas and big dreams and big visions for what lies ahead.

Spiked Satsuma Champagne,
Pickled Shrimp, Grits Crostini

Spiked Satsuma Champagne,
Southern 75

Bacon-Wrapped Bourbon Figs

Pickled Shrimp,
Grits Crostini

Parmesan-Crusted Crab Cake Bites with
Chive Aïoli, Asparagus with Curry Dip

Raspberry Panna Cotta

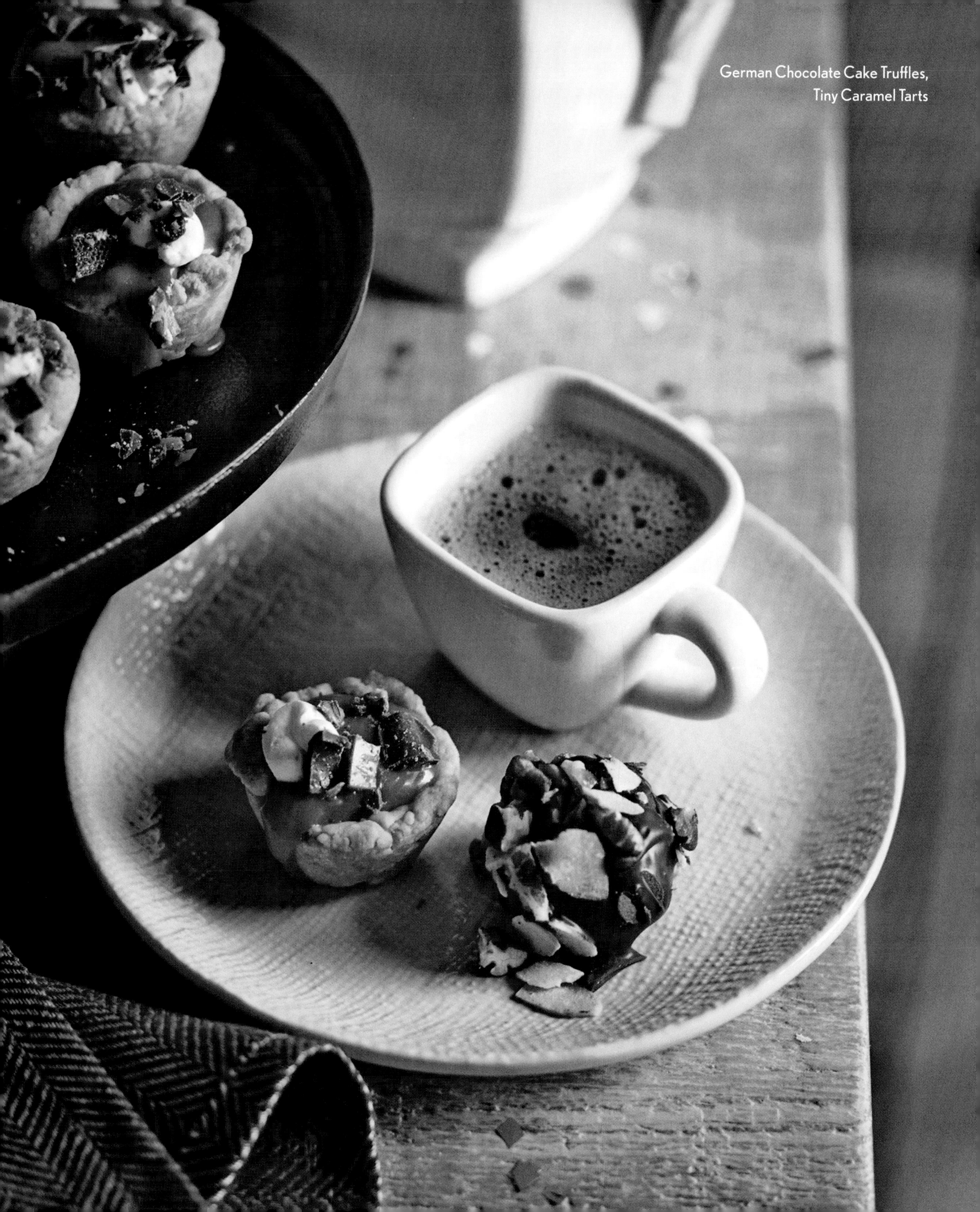

German Chocolate Cake Truffles,
Tiny Caramel Tarts

New Year's resolutions? I don't do those. Instead, every day I try to do better. See better. Say better. Talk better. Be better. I do my best. And I blow it 10 times out of 12. I ask forgiveness of anyone whose feelings I may have hurt. I ask forgiveness of God. I forgive myself. And then I start again.

—MAYA ANGELOU

NEW BEGINNINGS

For many folks, particularly those in the Lowcountry, it wouldn't be a proper New Year's Day without a lucky oyster roast. As winter breezes blow, rustling the amber marsh grass, tall pines, and moss-covered oaks, they also carry the unmistakable aroma of a campfire.

❦

The process of roasting the oysters really begins just as the flames start to die down. Typically, the oysters are spread out in a single layer and covered with a soaking-wet burlap sack or thick towel to steam. The hot coals from the fire impart a subtle smokiness that transcends both the classic raw and steamed oyster experience.

FRESH FARE

Skidaway River is the backdrop for a fresh-air gathering to kick off the New Year. The island in Savannah, Georgia, is fittingly named Isle of Hope.

A FRESH
START

Come over for a little luck
and a lot of fun as we kick off
the New Year with a
traditional lucky oyster roast.

LUCKY OYSTER ROAST

Grilled Oysters with Sauce Trio

Cumin-Spiced Black-Eyed Pea Dip

Celery Root and Apple Slaw
with Citrus Dressing

Collard Green and Kale Salad

Warm Country Ham-Cream
Cheese Bites

Bourbon Ginger Punch

Lemon-Glazed Fried Cherry Pies

RECIPES ON PAGES 376-380

Bourbon Ginger Punch

A TROVE OF TRADITIONS

Of all the New Year's culinary customs, here's a final important tradition to keep in mind
as you prepare to indulge: Eat as much lucky food as possible, but be sure to leave some on your plate
and for leftovers. It's a token of frugality and increases your chances of prosperity in the coming year.

Grilled Oysters with Sauce Trio

Fresh Oysters

Celery Root and Apple Slaw
with Citrus Dressing

Lemon-Glazed
Fried Cherry Pies

Festive Recipes

A HEARTY
PICNIC IN
THE PINES

ROSEMARY-SCENTED
COLD CIDER

SKILLET FRIED CHICKEN

APPLE-CABBAGE SLAW

SWEET POTATO SALAD

CHAMELEON ICEBOX COOKIES

CARAMEL DROP-BANANA
BREAD TRIFLE DESSERT

ROSEMARY-SCENTED COLD CIDER

MAKES 9½ CUPS • HANDS-ON 5 MIN. • TOTAL 8 HR., 5 MIN.

Pick up a jug of fresh-pressed cider for optimum results with this refreshing drink.

- 5   cups apple cider
- 4   (4- to 5-inch) fresh rosemary sprigs
- 2   cups cranberry-apple juice drink, chilled
- 2   (12-oz.) cans ginger ale, chilled

1. Bring cider and 4 rosemary sprigs to a boil in a saucepan over medium-high heat. Reduce heat to medium-low; simmer 3 minutes. Remove from heat; let cool to room temperature. Cover and chill 8 to 24 hours. Remove and discard rosemary sprigs.

2. Combine cider and cranberry-apple drink in a pitcher or thermos. Add ginger ale just before serving.

SKILLET FRIED CHICKEN

MAKES 4 TO 6 SERVINGS • HANDS-ON 11 MIN. • TOTAL 2 HR., 37 MIN.

Enjoy this crispy, well-seasoned chicken hot from the skillet, or cool and chill it, and nibble on the road to Grandma's.

- 2   cups buttermilk
- ¼   cup dill pickle juice
- 1   Tbsp. chopped fresh rosemary
- ½   tsp. paprika
- ¼   tsp. ground red pepper
- 2   garlic cloves, pressed
- 1   (4-lb.) cut-up whole chicken
- 1   cup self-rising flour
- 1   Tbsp. plus 1 tsp. seasoned salt
- 2   tsp. freshly ground black pepper
- Peanut oil

1. Place 1 large zip-top plastic freezer bag inside another zip-top plastic freezer bag. Combine first 6 ingredients in the inside bag. Add chicken pieces, tossing to coat. Seal both bags, and chill at least 2 hours or overnight.

2. Remove chicken from marinade, discarding marinade. Combine flour, salt, and black pepper. Dredge chicken in flour mixture, shaking off excess.

3. Pour oil to depth of 1½ inches in a deep skillet or Dutch oven; heat to 350°. Add chicken, a few pieces at a time; cover and cook 6 minutes. Uncover chicken, and cook 9 minutes. Turn chicken; cover and cook 6 minutes. Uncover and cook 5 to 9 minutes, turning chicken the last 3 minutes for even browning, if necessary. Drain on paper towels. Serve immediately, or let cool; cover and chill.

Apple-Cabbage Slaw

MAKES 8 TO 10 SERVINGS · HANDS-ON 5 MIN. · TOTAL 5 MIN.

Adding dried fruit and nut mix to this slaw is an easy way to add color, flavor, and crunch in a single ingredient.

½	cup canola oil
3	Tbsp. apple cider vinegar
2	Tbsp. honey
½	tsp. table salt
⅛	tsp. freshly ground black pepper
1	(10-oz.) package finely shredded cabbage
1	cup dried fruit and nut mix
2	Fuji apples, cored and finely chopped
2	green onions, minced

1. Whisk together first 5 ingredients in a large bowl; add cabbage and remaining ingredients. Toss well. Cover and chill until ready to serve.

Sweet Potato Salad

MAKES 6 TO 8 SERVINGS · HANDS-ON 11 MIN. · TOTAL 56 MIN.

This salad is great warm or chilled. With honey-mustard undertones, it pairs well with fried chicken, turkey, or ham.

4	large sweet potatoes, peeled and cubed
1	Tbsp. olive oil
½	tsp. table salt
½	tsp. freshly ground black pepper
2	Tbsp. mustard seeds
¼	cup rice vinegar
3	Tbsp. honey
¼	tsp. ground cinnamon
¼	tsp. curry powder
¼	tsp. dry mustard

1. Preheat oven to 450°. Toss together sweet potatoes, oil, salt, and pepper on a lightly greased large rimmed baking sheet or roasting pan. Roast at 450° for 45 minutes or until potatoes are tender and lightly browned. (Do not stir.)

2. Meanwhile, toast mustard seeds in a small skillet over medium heat until fragrant, stirring or shaking skillet to prevent burning. Add vinegar, honey, and spices; bring to a boil. Remove from heat. Pour over sweet potatoes in a serving bowl; toss. Serve warm, or cover and chill.

Chameleon Icebox Cookies

MAKES ABOUT 4 DOZEN • HANDS-ON 18 MIN. • TOTAL 1 HR., 40 MIN.

Old-fashioned icebox cookies become a creative and tasty blank canvas for Christmas stir-ins. Our staff had a hard time choosing a favorite variation.

1   cup butter, softened
1   cup superfine sugar
1   large egg
2   tsp. vanilla extract
2¼   cups all-purpose flour
½   tsp. table salt
     Wax paper

1. Beat butter at medium speed with an electric mixer until creamy; gradually add sugar, beating well. Add egg and vanilla; beat well.

2. Combine flour and salt; add to butter mixture, beating at medium-low speed just until blended. Cover and chill dough at least 1 hour.

3. Shape dough into 2 (6-inch) logs. Wrap logs in wax paper or parchment paper; chill or freeze until firm.

4. Preheat oven to 350°. Slice dough into ¼-inch-thick slices. Place on ungreased baking sheets. Bake at 350° for 12 minutes or until barely golden. Remove to wire racks, and let cool completely (about 10 minutes).

VARIATIONS:

Bittersweet Chocolate & Orange Essence Icebox Cookies:

Stir ½ cup (4 oz.) finely chopped bittersweet chocolate and 1 Tbsp. orange zest into dough. Proceed with recipe as directed. Bake 12 to 13 minutes or until golden.

Strawberry-Pecan Icebox Cookies:

Stir ¾ cup finely chopped dried strawberries into dough. Roll logs in 1 cup finely chopped pecans. Proceed with recipe as directed.

Kids' Icebox Cookies:

Roll 1 log of dough in ⅓ cup green decorator sugar crystals. Roll remaining log in ⅓ cup red decorator sugar crystals. Proceed with recipe as directed.

Lavender Icebox Cookies:

Stir 1½ Tbsp. dried lavender, lightly crushed, into dough. Proceed with recipe as directed.

Note: We used a mini food chopper to crush the lavender.

Caramel Drop-Banana Bread Trifle Dessert

MAKES 8 TO 10 SERVINGS • HANDS-ON 30 MIN. • TOTAL 2 HR., 30 MIN.

Instead of using vanilla wafers in this yummy banana pudding dessert, we chopped a loaf of banana bread. Pick up a loaf at a local bakery or grocer's bakery section. Assemble this dessert in a large, shallow plastic container with a lid; chill and take it to a holiday gathering.

Custard

1	cup sugar
2/3	cup all-purpose flour
1/2	tsp. table salt
5	cups milk
5	large egg yolks
1	Tbsp. vanilla extract
1	Tbsp. butter

Trifle Dessert

1	(1-lb.) banana bread loaf without nuts (about 8 x 4 inches)
2	large ripe bananas, sliced
1	(13.4-oz.) can dulce de leche
1	(8-oz.) container frozen whipped topping, thawed
1	cup chopped pecans, toasted

1. Prepare Custard: Combine first 3 ingredients in a heavy saucepan; whisk in milk. Cook over medium heat, stirring constantly, until thickened and bubbly (about 12 minutes).

2. Whisk egg yolks until thick and pale. Gradually stir about one-fourth of hot mixture into yolks; add yolk mixture to remaining hot mixture, stirring constantly. Cook over medium heat, stirring gently, 3 minutes. Remove from heat; add vanilla and butter, stirring until butter melts. Place plastic wrap directly onto warm custard (to prevent a film from forming). Cool to room temperature. Cover and chill up to a day ahead. (Custard will be thick.)

3. Prepare Trifle Dessert: Chop banana bread loaf into 3/4-inch pieces to yield about 5 cups. Place banana bread pieces in a 13- x 9-inch baking dish or similar-size heavy-duty plastic container. Spoon and spread Custard over banana bread; top with banana slices. Top dessert with small dollops of dulce de leche. Top with whipped topping, spreading to edges; sprinkle with pecans. Cover and chill 1 to 24 hours.

A CASUAL COCKTAIL SUPPER

Perfect Beef Tenderloin

Homemade Hot Mustard

Horseradish Sauce

Montgomery Punch

Ice Ring

Cheese Dreams

Asparagus with Curry Dip (page 373)

Mini Corn Cakes with Smoked Salmon and Dill Crème Fraîche

Lump Crab Mornay

Cheese Spread

Buttery Toasted Pecans

Pecan Bourbon Balls

PERFECT BEEF TENDERLOIN

MAKES 12 TO 14 APPETIZER SERVINGS · HANDS-ON 10 MIN. · TOTAL 50 MIN.

When seasoning roasts, this will generally do the trick: 1 tsp. of kosher salt per pound of meat. Plan on about 5 pounds of meat for every 12 guests.

1   (5- to 7-lb.) beef tenderloin, trimmed
3   Tbsp. butter, softened
5   to 7 tsp. kosher salt
3/4   tsp. cracked black pepper

1. Preheat oven to 425°. Place beef on a wire rack in a jelly-roll pan. Rub butter over beef, and sprinkle with salt and pepper.

2. Bake at 425° for 25 to 35 minutes or until a meat thermometer inserted into thickest portion registers 135° (medium rare). Cover loosely with aluminum foil; let stand 15 minutes before slicing.

Note: We tested with Diamond Crystal Kosher Salt.

HOMEMADE HOT MUSTARD

MAKES 2 1/4 CUPS · HANDS-ON 20 MIN. · TOTAL 13 HR., 20 MIN.

In Greenville, Mississippi, this mustard is golden. It's been passed from one kitchen to another for decades.

1   cup dry mustard
1   cup apple cider vinegar
1   cup sugar
3   large pasteurized eggs, lightly beaten

1. Stir together first 2 ingredients in top of a double boiler. Cover and let stand 12 to 24 hours.

2. Pour water to depth of 1 inch into bottom of a double boiler over medium-high heat; bring to a boil. Reduce heat to low, and simmer; place top of double boiler over simmering water. Whisk sugar and eggs into mustard mixture, and cook, whisking constantly, 8 to 10 minutes or until thickened. Remove from heat, and cool completely (about 1 hour). (Mixture will continue to thicken as it cools.) Refrigerate in an airtight container up to 2 weeks.

Note: We tested with Colman's Mustard Powder.

HORSERADISH SAUCE

MAKES ABOUT 2 CUPS • HANDS-ON 5 MIN. • TOTAL 5 MIN.

Give this classic tenderloin condiment as much horseradish oomph as you please.

1⅓ cups sour cream
½ cup whipping cream, whipped to soft peaks
6 Tbsp. prepared horseradish
1½ tsp. Dijon mustard
2 to 3 tsp. fresh lemon juice
½ tsp. sugar

1. Fold together first 4 ingredients in a medium bowl. Stir in lemon juice and sugar. Add salt and pepper to taste.

MONTGOMERY PUNCH

MAKES 14 CUPS • HANDS-ON 15 MIN. • TOTAL 9 HR., 40 MIN., INCLUDING ICE RING

Julia found this recipe in a cookbook by the Junior League of Montgomery, Alabama, where the punch is a town staple.

2 cups fresh lemon juice
1½ cups sugar
1 cup brandy
Ice Ring
2 (750-milliliter) bottles chilled sparkling wine
1 (375-milliliter) bottle chilled dessert wine (such as Sauternes)
Garnishes: orange slices, lemon slices, cranberries

1. Stir together first 2 ingredients until sugar dissolves. Stir in brandy. Pour over Ice Ring in a punch bowl. Stir in sparkling and dessert wines.

ICE RING

MAKES 1 ICE RING • HANDS-ON 5 MIN. • TOTAL 9 HR., 25 MIN.

Freeze 3 cups water in a tube pan or Bundt pan (that will fit into a punch bowl) 4 hours or until set. Place sliced fruit, such as lemons and oranges, in a single layer over ice, and freeze 1 hour. Remove from freezer; let stand 10 minutes. Add 5 cups ice-cold water; freeze 4 hours or until set. Let stand at room temperature 10 minutes before unmolding.

CHEESE DREAMS

MAKES ABOUT 3 DOZEN • HANDS-ON 30 MIN. • TOTAL 45 MIN.

These little gems will be the first appetizer to disappear. Make them the day before and refrigerate, or freeze up to 3 weeks. If frozen, pop in the oven straight from the freezer; increase the bake time by 10 minutes.

2 cups finely grated sharp Cheddar cheese
1 cup butter, softened
2 Tbsp. heavy cream
1 large egg
1 tsp. Worcestershire sauce
½ tsp. table salt
½ tsp. dry mustard
Ground red pepper or hot sauce to taste
1 (16-oz.) package firm white sandwich bread slices

1. Preheat oven to 375°. Beat cheese and butter at medium speed with an electric mixer until blended. Beat in cream and next 5 ingredients.

2. Cut crusts from bread slices; cut each bread slice into 4 squares. Spread cheese mixture on half of bread squares (about 1 tsp. per square); top each with 1 remaining square. Spread remaining cheese mixture over top and sides of sandwiches. Place sandwiches, 1 inch apart, on a lightly greased baking sheet.

3. Bake at 375° for 15 minutes or until golden brown.

Note: We tested with Pepperidge Farm White Sandwich Bread.

Mini Corn Cakes with Smoked Salmon and Dill Crème Fraîche

MAKES 2 DOZEN • HANDS-ON 20 MIN. • TOTAL 50 MIN.

Make these in the morning, and top with salmon and crème fraîche just before your guests arrive. Tight on time? Use store-bought blini instead.

1   (8.25-oz.) can cream-style corn

1   cup plain white cornmeal

1   cup sour cream

2   Tbsp. vegetable oil

1½   tsp. baking powder

1   tsp. table salt

2   large eggs

1   cup crème fraîche

2   Tbsp. finely chopped fresh dill weed

1   Tbsp. fresh lemon juice

2   (4-oz.) packages thinly sliced smoked salmon, flaked

1. Preheat oven to 350°. Whisk together first 7 ingredients until smooth. Spoon 1 heaping teaspoonful corn mixture into each cup of a well-greased 24-cup miniature muffin pan.

2. Bake at 350° for 20 minutes. Cool 10 minutes.

3. Stir together crème fraîche, dill, and lemon juice. Top muffins with crème fraîche and salmon.

Lump Crab Mornay

MAKES 10 TO 12 SERVINGS • HANDS-ON 20 MIN. • TOTAL 20 MIN.

Julia adapted this creamy dip from a recipe in Bayou Cuisine *by St. Stephen's Episcopal Church in Indianola, Mississippi.*

½   cup butter, softened

1   bunch green onions, chopped

2   Tbsp. all-purpose flour

2   cups heavy cream

1   cup freshly grated Gruyère or Swiss cheese

2   Tbsp. dry sherry

¼   tsp. kosher salt

¼   tsp. ground red pepper

1   lb. fresh jumbo lump crabmeat

½   cup chopped fresh flat-leaf parsley

Store-bought or homemade toast points

1. Melt butter in a heavy saucepan over medium-high heat; add onions, and sauté 3 minutes or until tender. Whisk in flour, and cook, whisking constantly, 2 minutes. Add cream, and cook, whisking constantly, until smooth and sauce begins to bubble. Remove from heat, and stir in cheese until smooth. Stir in sherry, salt, and pepper. Gently fold in crabmeat and parsley. Keep warm in a chafing dish or slow cooker set on WARM or LOW. Serve with toast points.

CHEESE SPREAD

MAKES ABOUT 1¼ CUPS • HANDS-ON 10 MIN. • TOTAL 2 HR., 10 MIN.

Inspired by a recipe from Julia Child, this sharp, tangy spread can turn a celery stick into an unforgettable appetizer.

½ (8-oz.) package cream cheese, softened
¼ cup butter, softened
4 oz. Roquefort or other blue cheese, crumbled
1½ Tbsp. minced fresh chives
1 Tbsp. minced celery
1 Tbsp. cognac
⅛ tsp. ground red pepper
⅛ tsp. freshly ground pepper
Assorted crackers and sliced fresh vegetables

1. Beat cream cheese and butter at medium speed with a heavy-duty electric stand mixer until smooth. Beat in blue cheese and next 5 ingredients on low speed until blended. Spoon into a serving bowl. Chill 2 hours. Serve with crackers and vegetables.

BUTTERY TOASTED PECANS

MAKES 4 CUPS • HANDS-ON 10 MIN. • TOTAL 35 MIN.

Patiently roasting pecans (the entire 25 minutes!) at 325° to coax out their flavor and essential oils takes them from good to great.

¼ cup butter, melted
4 cups pecan halves
1 Tbsp. kosher salt
½ tsp. ground red pepper

1. Preheat oven to 325°. Toss together butter and pecans. Spread pecans in a single layer in a jelly-roll pan; bake 25 minutes or until toasted and fragrant, stirring halfway through. Remove from oven, and sprinkle with salt and pepper, tossing to coat. Cool completely. Store up to 1 week.

PECAN BOURBON BALLS

MAKES ABOUT 3½ DOZEN • HANDS-ON 30 MIN. • TOTAL 30 MIN.

Enhance the flavor of bourbon balls by coating them in spiced toasted pecans for a sweet-salty variation and you'll be a convert for life.

1 (12-oz.) package vanilla wafers, finely crushed
1 cup powdered sugar
1 cup finely chopped toasted pecans
½ cup bourbon
2 Tbsp. unsweetened cocoa
2 Tbsp. light corn syrup
Powdered sugar
Buttery Toasted Pecans, coarsely chopped (recipe at left)

1. Stir together first 6 ingredients. Shape into 1-inch balls. Roll in powdered sugar or pecans. Refrigerate up to 2 weeks.

SUPPER BY THE SEA

ORANGE THING PUNCH

BENNE SEED CHEESE WAFERS

SHRIMP AND ANDOUILLE
SAUSAGE OVER PARMESAN GRITS

GARLIC ROASTED
ASPARAGUS

WHITE CHOCOLATE-
CRANBERRY CRÈME BRÛLÉE

ORANGE THING PUNCH

MAKES ABOUT 8 CUPS · HANDS-ON 10 MIN. · TOTAL 9 HR., 10 MIN.

2½   cups vodka
1¼   cups orange liqueur
4   cups fresh orange juice
14   (2½-inch) pieces orange peel
4   (8-inch-long) wooden skewers
Wax paper

1. Stir together vodka, orange liqueur, and orange juice in a pitcher. Cover and refrigerate up to 2 days ahead.

2. Twist orange peel around wooden skewers, and place on wax paper. Let stand 1 hour.

3. Fill each compartment of desired ice cube trays with water and an orange twist. Freeze 8 hours or until firm.

4. Serve punch over prepared ice cubes in Collins glasses.

Note: We used Cointreau for orange liqueur.

VARIATION:

SPARKLING ORANGE THING PUNCH

Prepare recipe as directed, omitting ice cubes. Serve punch in Champagne flutes, and top with desired amount of Prosecco or Champagne.

Shrimp and Andouille Sausage over Parmesan Grits

MAKES 8 TO 10 SERVINGS · HANDS-ON 35 MIN. · TOTAL 1 HR., 10 MIN., INCLUDING GRITS

- 1 (16-oz.) package andouille sausage, sliced
- 1 Tbsp. butter
- 1 large sweet onion, chopped
- 1 red bell pepper, chopped
- 3 garlic cloves, minced
- ⅓ cup white wine
- 1 cup whipping cream
- 3 lb. large raw shrimp, peeled and deveined, if desired
- ½ tsp. Creole seasoning
- 3 Tbsp. chopped fresh parsley

Parmesan Grits

Chopped fresh parsley

1. Cook sausage in a large skillet 10 minutes, stirring frequently, or until browned. Drain sausage, reserving 2 Tbsp. drippings in skillet.

2. Melt butter in skillet; add onion and pepper, and cook 10 minutes, stirring often.

3. Add garlic, and cook 1 minute. Add wine, and cook 2 minutes, stirring to loosen browned bits from bottom of skillet.

4. Add whipping cream and next 3 ingredients. Cook 5 minutes or just until shrimp turn pink and sauce thickens slightly. Season to taste with salt and pepper. Serve over Parmesan Grits, and sprinkle with parsley just before serving.

Parmesan Grits

MAKES 8 TO 10 SERVINGS · HANDS-ON 35 MIN. · TOTAL 35 MIN.

- 4 cups milk
- 1½ tsp. table salt
- 2 cups uncooked stone-ground white grits
- 1 cup grated Parmesan cheese
- 2 Tbsp. butter

1. Combine milk and 4 cups water in a large Dutch oven. Bring to a boil over high heat; add salt. Gradually whisk in grits. Reduce heat, and simmer 25 minutes or until thickened, whisking often.

2. Remove from heat; stir in Parmesan cheese and butter. Season to taste with salt and pepper.

Benne Seed Cheese Wafers

MAKES ABOUT 4 DOZEN · HANDS-ON 15 MIN. · TOTAL 27 MIN.

Sesame seeds are called benne seeds in the southeastern coastal plains region of Georgia and South Carolina's Lowcountry. You can purchase toasted sesame seeds, but for the most flavor, toast your own at 350° for 5 minutes, stirring occasionally.

- 1 cup all-purpose flour
- ⅓ cup toasted sesame seeds
- ½ tsp. table salt
- ¼ tsp. dry mustard
- ½ cup butter, softened
- 1 (8-oz.) block sharp Cheddar cheese, shredded
- ½ cup toasted sesame seeds (optional)

1. Preheat oven to 350°. Stir together first 4 ingredients in a small bowl.

2. Beat butter at medium speed with an electric mixer until creamy. Add cheese, and beat just until blended. Gradually add flour mixture, beating just until dry ingredients are moistened and a dough forms.

3. Roll dough into 1-inch balls. Roll balls in additional sesame seeds, if desired, pressing gently into dough. Place balls 2 inches apart on ungreased baking sheets; flatten to ⅛-inch thickness with bottom of a glass.

4. Bake at 350° for 12 minutes or until edges are lightly browned.

Garlic Roasted Asparagus

MAKES 8 TO 10 SERVINGS · HANDS-ON 10 MIN. · TOTAL 22 MIN.

3   lb. fresh asparagus

3   Tbsp. olive oil

2   to 3 garlic cloves, minced

1½ tsp. kosher salt

½   tsp. freshly ground black pepper

1   tsp. lemon zest

1. Preheat oven to 350°. Snap off and discard tough ends of asparagus; place on a large rimmed baking sheet. Drizzle with olive oil. Sprinkle with garlic, salt, and pepper, tossing to coat.

2. Bake at 350° for 12 to 15 minutes or just until tender. Transfer to a serving dish, and sprinkle with lemon zest.

White Chocolate-Cranberry Crème Brûlée

MAKES 6 SERVINGS · HANDS-ON 30 MIN. · TOTAL 9 HR., 48 MIN.

2   cups whipping cream

4   oz. white chocolate

1   tsp. vanilla extract

5   large egg yolks

½   cup sugar, divided

½   (14-oz.) can whole-berry cranberry sauce

    Ice cubes

1. Preheat oven to 300°. Combine ½ cup cream and chocolate in a heavy saucepan; cook over low heat, stirring constantly, 2 to 3 minutes or until chocolate is melted. Remove from heat. Stir in vanilla and remaining 1½ cups cream.

2. Whisk together egg yolks and ¼ cup sugar until sugar is dissolved and mixture is thick and pale yellow. Add cream mixture, whisking until well blended. Pour mixture through a fine wire-mesh strainer into a large bowl.

3. Spoon 1½ Tbsp. cranberry sauce into each of 6 (4-oz.) ramekins. Pour cream mixture into ramekins; place ramekins in a large roasting pan. Add water to pan to depth of ½ inch.

4. Bake at 300° for 45 to 55 minutes or until edges are set. Cool custards in pan on a wire rack 25 minutes. Remove ramekins from water; cover and chill 8 hours.

5. Preheat broiler with oven rack 5 inches from heat. Sprinkle remaining ¼ cup sugar over ramekins. Fill a large roasting pan or 15- x 10-inch jelly-roll pan with ice; arrange ramekins in pan.

6. Broil 3 to 5 minutes or until sugar is melted and caramelized. Let stand 5 minutes.

Tip: Filling the roasting pan with ice before broiling keeps the custards cool while caramelizing the tops.

A YULETIDE FEAST

Sweet Potato Soup

Arugula-Pear-Blue
Cheese Salad

Cranberry Roasted
Winter Vegetables

Pork Roast with
Sweet Onion-Pumpkin
Seed Relish

Wild Rice with Bacon
and Fennel

Gingerbread Soufflés

Sweet Potato Soup

MAKES 8 CUPS • HANDS-ON 35 MIN. • TOTAL 1 HR., 5 MIN.

Make the soup through Step 2 the day before. Reheat and stir in the lime juice before serving.

2	Tbsp. butter
1	medium onion, chopped
2	garlic cloves, minced
5½	cups reduced-sodium fat-free chicken broth
2	lb. sweet potatoes, peeled and chopped (2 large)
1	cup apple cider
1	tsp. minced canned chipotle pepper in adobo sauce
1	tsp. table salt
2	Tbsp. fresh lime juice
½	cup sour cream
2	tsp. fresh lime juice

Garnish: fresh cilantro

1. Melt butter in a large saucepan over medium-high heat; add onion, and sauté 5 to 7 minutes or until tender. Add garlic; sauté 1 minute. Stir in broth and next 4 ingredients. Bring to a boil; reduce heat to medium-low, and simmer 20 minutes or until potatoes are tender.

2. Process mixture with a handheld blender until smooth. (If you don't have a handheld blender, cool mixture 10 minutes, and process, in batches, in a regular blender until smooth. Return to saucepan, and proceed with Step 3.)

3. Cook potato mixture over low heat, stirring occasionally, 5 minutes or until thoroughly heated. Stir in 2 Tbsp. lime juice. Whisk together sour cream and 2 tsp. lime juice. Ladle soup into bowls, and drizzle each serving with sour cream mixture.

ARUGULA-PEAR-BLUE CHEESE SALAD

MAKES 8 SERVINGS · HANDS-ON 15 MIN. · TOTAL 15 MIN.

¼   cup plus 2 Tbsp. pear preserves

½   cup Champagne vinegar

1   shallot, sliced

2   tsp. Dijon mustard

½   tsp. table salt

¼   tsp. freshly ground black pepper

½   cup olive oil

8   cups loosely packed arugula

2   Bartlett pears, cut into 6 wedges each

4   oz. blue cheese, crumbled

¼   cup chopped toasted walnuts

1. Process ¼ cup preserves and next 5 ingredients in a food processor 30 seconds to 1 minute or until smooth. With processor running, pour oil through food chute in a slow, steady stream, processing until smooth. Transfer to a 2-cup measuring cup or small bowl, and stir in remaining 2 Tbsp. pear preserves.

2. Place arugula in a large serving bowl. Top with pears, blue cheese, and walnuts. Drizzle with vinaigrette.

CRANBERRY ROASTED WINTER VEGETABLES

MAKES 8 SERVINGS · HANDS-ON 30 MIN. · TOTAL 1 HR., 20 MIN.

Roast the vegetables before the pork roast. Then, put them back in the oven to reheat while the pork rests.

4   large carrots (about 1½ lb.), halved lengthwise and cut into 1-inch pieces

3   large turnips (about 2 lb.), peeled and cut into 1-inch pieces*

1   lb. Brussels sprouts, halved (quartered, if large)

1   Tbsp. minced fresh rosemary

2   Tbsp. olive oil

¾   tsp. table salt

¼   tsp. freshly ground black pepper

1   cup fresh or thawed frozen cranberries

4   tsp. molasses

1. Preheat oven to 400°. Lightly grease 2 large jelly-roll pans; place carrots and turnips in 1 pan and Brussels sprouts in second pan. Divide rosemary and next 3 ingredients between carrot mixture and Brussels sprouts; toss each to coat.

2. Bake both pans at 400° at the same time. Bake carrot mixture 30 minutes, stirring once; add cranberries, and bake 5 minutes or until carrots and turnips are tender and browned and cranberries begin to soften. Bake Brussels sprouts 15 to 20 minutes or until tender and browned, stirring once.

3. Remove vegetables from oven, and combine in a large serving bowl. Drizzle with molasses, and toss to coat.

*2 lb. parsnips may be substituted.

Pork Roast with Sweet Onion-Pumpkin Seed Relish

MAKES 8 SERVINGS · HANDS-ON 20 MIN. · TOTAL 1 HR., 50 MIN.

Be sure to ask your butcher to cut out the chine bone and to french the rib rack for easy carving and an elegant presentation.

1¼   tsp. table salt, divided
½   tsp. freshly ground black pepper
1   (5-lb.) 8-rib bone-in pork loin roast, chine bone removed
1   Tbsp. minced fresh rosemary
4   tsp. minced fresh thyme, divided
3   large sweet onions (about 2 lb.), cut into ½-inch-thick rings
2   Tbsp. olive oil
⅛   tsp. freshly ground black pepper
1   tsp. white wine vinegar
1   tsp. light brown sugar
¼   cup toasted pumpkin seeds

1. Preheat oven to 450°. Sprinkle 1 tsp. salt and ½ tsp. pepper over pork; rub rosemary and 1 Tbsp. thyme over pork. Place pork in a lightly greased roasting pan.

2. Toss together onions, olive oil, ⅛ tsp. pepper, and remaining ¼ tsp. salt until coated. Arrange onions around pork.

3. Bake at 450° for 30 minutes; reduce oven temperature to 375°. Bake 50 more minutes or until a meat thermometer inserted into thickest portion registers 145°, stirring onions once. Transfer pork to a cutting board; cover loosely with aluminum foil, and let stand 10 minutes before slicing.

4. Meanwhile, coarsely chop onions; transfer to a bowl. Stir in vinegar, brown sugar, and remaining 1 tsp. thyme. Stir in pumpkin seeds before serving. Serve pork with relish.

Wild Rice with Bacon and Fennel

MAKES 8 SERVINGS · HANDS-ON 40 MIN. · TOTAL 1 HR., 5 MIN.

Use wild rice, not a blend, for the best texture.

1⅓   cups uncooked wild rice
4   bacon slices
1   large fennel bulb, thinly sliced
1   large onion, cut into thin wedges
2   garlic cloves, minced
½   cup reduced-sodium fat-free chicken broth
⅓   cup golden raisins
¼   tsp. table salt
⅛   tsp. freshly ground black pepper
¼   cup chopped fresh fennel fronds or flat-leaf parsley
1   Tbsp. white wine vinegar
½   cup chopped toasted walnuts

1. Cook wild rice according to package directions; drain.

2. Meanwhile, cook bacon in a large nonstick skillet over medium-high heat 7 to 8 minutes or until crisp; drain on paper towels, reserving 1 Tbsp. drippings in skillet. Chop bacon.

3. Sauté fennel bulb and onion in hot drippings over medium-high heat 5 minutes or until softened. Add garlic;

sauté 1 minute. Add broth and next 3 ingredients; bring to a boil. Reduce heat to medium-low; cover and simmer 8 minutes or until tender. Stir in rice and bacon; cook, stirring often, 3 minutes.

4. Transfer to a large serving bowl. Stir in fennel fronds and vinegar. Stir in walnuts just before serving.

Gingerbread Soufflés

MAKES 10 SERVINGS · HANDS-ON 20 MIN. · TOTAL 1 HR.

This impressive dessert isn't difficult, but do plan ahead. Preheat the oven, and just before sitting down to dinner, pop the soufflés in. When done, serve them all puffed up and gorgeous.

1	cup milk
½	cup sugar
¼	cup all-purpose flour
¼	tsp. table salt
⅓	cup molasses
2	Tbsp. butter, softened
2	tsp. pumpkin pie spice
1	tsp. ground ginger
2	tsp. vanilla extract
6	large eggs, separated
⅛	tsp. cream of tartar

Sweetened whipped cream, crushed gingersnaps

1. Preheat oven to 350°. Whisk together first 4 ingredients in a medium saucepan until smooth. Bring to a boil over medium heat, whisking constantly. Transfer mixture to a large bowl, and whisk in molasses and next 4 ingredients. Cool 15 minutes. Whisk in egg yolks.

2. Butter 10 (7-oz.) ramekins; sprinkle with sugar to coat, and shake out excess.

3. Beat egg whites and cream of tartar at high speed with an electric mixer until stiff peaks form. Fold one-third of egg white mixture into milk mixture until well blended. Repeat twice with remaining egg white mixture. Spoon batter into prepared ramekins, leaving ¾-inch space at top of each.

4. Bake at 350° for 25 minutes or until puffy and set. Serve immediately with whipped cream and crushed gingersnaps.

Tip: You may also bake this in a 2½-qt. soufflé dish. Bake 55 to 60 minutes or until puffy and set.

COOKIES & COCKTAILS

GINGERBREAD
LINZER COOKIES

SPICED SORGHUM SNOWFLAKES

ALMOND POINSETTIA COOKIES

COCONUT SNOWBALLS

SPARKLING CRANBERRY CIDER

CHOCOLATE CREAM MARTINI

CARAMEL APPLE CIDER

GINGERBREAD LINZER COOKIES

MAKES 2 DOZEN SANDWICH COOKIES • HANDS-ON 30 MIN. •
TOTAL 4 HR.

Gingerbread dough is rolled and cut to resemble traditional Austrian Linzer cookies, only with festive bell-shaped centers and a lemon curd filling.

³/₄	cup butter, softened
1	cup firmly packed light brown sugar
¹/₂	cup molasses
1	large egg
3	cups all-purpose flour
1	tsp. baking soda
2	tsp. ground ginger
2	tsp. ground cinnamon
¹/₂	tsp. table salt
¹/₂	tsp. ground cloves
¹/₄	cup lemon curd or orange marmalade
Powdered sugar	

1. Beat butter at medium speed with an electric mixer until creamy; gradually add brown sugar, beating until blended. Add molasses and egg, beating just until blended.

2. Stir together flour and next 5 ingredients; gradually add to butter mixture, beating at low speed after each addition. Divide dough into 2 equal portions; flatten each into a disk. Cover and chill 3 hours.

3. Preheat oven to 350°. Place 1 portion of dough on a lightly floured surface, and roll to ¹/₈-inch thickness. Cut with a 2¹/₂-inch fluted round cutter. Place cookies 2 inches apart on lightly greased baking sheets. Repeat procedure with remaining dough disk. Cut centers out of half of cookies with a 1¹/₂-inch bell-shaped cutter. Place cookies 2 inches apart on lightly greased baking sheets.

4. Bake at 350° for 8 to 10 minutes or until edges are set. Cool on baking sheets 2 minutes. Transfer to wire racks, and cool completely (about 20 minutes).

5. Spread each solid cookie with ¹/₂ tsp. lemon curd. Sprinkle cookies with cutouts with powdered sugar. Top each solid cookie with a cookie with cutout.

Spiced Sorghum Snowflakes

MAKES ABOUT 7 DOZEN · HANDS-ON 3 HR., 25 MIN. · TOTAL 6 HR., 24 MIN., INCLUDING ICING

Perfect for gift giving or tucking inside a stocking, these beautiful crisp cookies are flavored with sorghum syrup and a blend of gingerbread spices.

- ½   cup butter, softened
- ¼   cup granulated sugar
- ¼   cup firmly packed dark brown sugar
- 2   tsp. orange zest
- 1   large egg
- 3   Tbsp. hot water
- 1   tsp. baking soda
- ½   cup sorghum syrup
- 3   cups all-purpose flour
- 2   tsp. ground ginger
- 1   tsp. ground cinnamon
- ½   tsp. ground allspice
- ¼   tsp. ground nutmeg
- ¼   tsp. table salt
-    Parchment paper
-    Royal Icing
-    White sparkling sugar, nonpareils, sugar pearls

1. Beat butter and sugars at medium speed with a heavy-duty electric stand mixer until fluffy. Add orange zest and egg, beating until smooth.

2. Stir together hot water and baking soda in a small bowl until baking soda is dissolved. Stir in sorghum syrup.

3. Stir together flour and next 5 ingredients; add to butter mixture alternately with sorghum syrup mixture, beginning and ending with flour mixture.

4. Divide dough into 2 equal portions; flatten each into a disk. Cover and chill at least 1 hour or until firm.

5. Preheat oven to 325°. Place 1 portion of dough on a lightly floured surface, and roll to ¼-inch thickness. Cut with assorted sizes of snowflake-shaped cutters. Place cookies 1 inch apart on parchment paper-lined baking sheets. Repeat procedure with remaining dough disk. (Once cookies are cut and placed on baking sheets, place in freezer. Freezing them about 10 minutes allows them to better hold their shape during baking.)

6. Bake at 325° for 13 to 15 minutes or until cookies are puffed and slightly darker around the edges. Cool on pans 1 minute; transfer to wire racks, and cool completely (about 30 minutes).

7. Spoon Royal Icing into a zip-top plastic freezer bag. Snip 1 corner of bag to make a small hole. Pipe icing in decorative designs on each cookie. Sprinkle with white sparkling sugar, and decorate with nonpareils and sugar pearls. Let icing harden at least 1 hour.

Note: We tested with snowflake-shaped cutters ranging in size from 1¾ inch to 4 inches.

Royal Icing

MAKES 3 CUPS · HANDS-ON 5 MIN. · TOTAL 5 MIN.

- 1   (16-oz.) package powdered sugar
- 3   Tbsp. meringue powder
- ½   cup warm water

1. Beat all ingredients at low speed with an electric mixer until blended. Beat at high speed 4 minutes or until glossy and stiff peaks form, adding a few drops of additional warm water, if necessary, for desired consistency.

ALMOND POINSETTIA COOKIES

MAKES ABOUT 2½ DOZEN • HANDS-ON 1 HR. • TOTAL 4 HR., 55 MIN., INCLUDING ICING

This recipe bakes up into pretty flower shapes that are ready for decorating. Shop online for a poinsettia cookie cutter.

2	cups all-purpose flour
½	cup almond flour
¼	tsp. table salt
¾	cup butter, softened
2	oz. cream cheese, softened
2	oz. almond paste
1	cup granulated sugar
1	large egg yolk
1	tsp. almond extract
	Royal Red Icing
¼	cup yellow candy sprinkles
¼	cup fine red sanding sugar

1. Combine first 3 ingredients in a small bowl. Beat butter and cream cheese at medium speed with an electric mixer until creamy. Add almond paste and granulated sugar, beating until light and fluffy. Add egg yolk and almond extract, beating just until blended. Gradually add flour mixture to cream cheese mixture, beating just until blended after each addition.

2. Divide dough into 2 equal portions; flatten each into a disk. Cover and chill 2 hours.

3. Preheat oven to 350°. Place 1 portion of dough on a lightly floured surface, and roll to ¼-inch thickness. Cut with a 3½- to 4-inch poinsettia-shaped cookie cutter. Place cookies 1 inch apart on ungreased baking sheets. Repeat procedure with remaining dough disk.

4. Bake at 350° for 13 to 15 minutes or until edges are golden brown. Cool on baking sheets 2 minutes. Transfer to wire racks, and cool completely (about 30 minutes).

5. Spoon Royal Red Icing into a small zip-top plastic freezer bag. Snip 1 corner of bag to make a small hole. Working with 1 cookie at a time, pipe icing to outline cookie. Use icing to fill in cookie. Lightly sprinkle yellow candies in center. Sprinkle petals with red sugar. Let icing harden at least 1 hour.

ROYAL RED ICING

MAKES ABOUT 3 CUPS • HANDS-ON 10 MIN. • TOTAL 10 MIN.

1	(16-oz.) package powdered sugar
3	Tbsp. meringue powder
¾	tsp. red paste food color
4	to 6 Tbsp. warm water

1. Beat first 3 ingredients and 4 Tbsp. warm water at low speed with an electric mixer until blended. Add up to 2 Tbsp. more water, 1 tsp. at a time, until desired consistency is reached.

Note: Royal icing dries rapidly. Work quickly, keeping extra icing tightly covered at all times. Place a damp paper towel directly on surface of icing (to prevent a crust from forming) while icing cookies.

COCONUT SNOWBALLS

MAKES ABOUT 4 DOZEN • HANDS-ON 20 MIN. • TOTAL 2 HR., 16 MIN.

1	cup sweetened flaked coconut
1	cup butter, softened
2	cups all-purpose flour
1¼	cups powdered sugar, divided
1	tsp. coconut extract
1	tsp. vanilla extract

1. Preheat oven to 350°. Place coconut in a single layer in a shallow pan.

2. Bake at 350° for 5 to 6 minutes or until toasted, stirring occasionally. Cool completely.

3. Beat butter at medium speed with an electric mixer 2 minutes or until light and fluffy. Gradually add flour and ½ cup powdered sugar, beating until blended. Add extracts, beating until blended. Stir in coconut. Cover and chill dough 1 hour.

4. Preheat oven to 350°. Shape dough into ¾-inch balls; place 1 inch apart on ungreased baking sheets. Bake at 350° for 16 to 18 minutes or until bottoms are golden brown. Cool on baking sheets 5 minutes.

5. Place remaining ¾ cup powdered sugar in a bowl. Roll warm cookies in powdered sugar, tossing to coat. Transfer to wire racks, and cool completely (about 30 minutes).

SPARKLING CRANBERRY CIDER

MAKES 8 TO 10 SERVINGS • HANDS-ON 7 MIN. • TOTAL 37 MIN.

Be sure to add the sparkling cider just before serving so that it doesn't lose its fizz.

- 1/2 tsp. ground ginger
- 1/2 tsp. orange zest
- 1/4 tsp. ground cloves
- 1 (12-oz.) can frozen cranberry juice cocktail
- 1 (3-inch) cinnamon stick
- 2 (750-milliliter) bottles sparkling apple cider, chilled

1. Place first 5 ingredients in a small saucepan. Bring to a boil over medium-high heat, stirring until cranberry juice cocktail melts. Remove from heat; let cool 30 minutes.

2. Pour cranberry juice mixture into a pitcher. Add cider, and stir gently. Serve over ice. Serve immediately.

CHOCOLATE CREAM MARTINI

MAKES 2 SERVINGS • HANDS-ON 10 MIN. • TOTAL 10 MIN.

This luxurious drink is both cocktail and dessert.

- 1 (1-oz.) square semisweet chocolate, melted
- 3 Tbsp. vanilla-flavored vodka
- 3 Tbsp. Irish cream liqueur
- 2 Tbsp. half-and-half
- 1/3 cup coffee liqueur
- 1/3 cup chocolate liqueur

1. Dip rims of 2 martini glasses in melted chocolate on a plate to form a thin layer. Place glasses in refrigerator until chocolate is firm.

2. Combine vodka and next 4 ingredients in a cocktail shaker filled with ice. Cover with lid; shake vigorously until thoroughly chilled (about 30 seconds). Strain into chocolate-rimmed martini glasses. Serve immediately.

Note: We tested with Absolut Vanilla vodka, Tia Maria coffee liqueur, and Godiva chocolate liqueur.

CARAMEL APPLE CIDER

MAKES 4 1/2 CUPS • HANDS-ON 13 MIN. • TOTAL 13 MIN.

This kid-friendly cup of warmth tastes like liquid apple pie.

- 1/3 cup firmly packed light brown sugar
- 1/3 cup heavy whipping cream
- 1 tsp. vanilla extract
- 4 cups apple cider
- Garnishes: whipped cream, caramel sauce, ground cinnamon

1. Stir together brown sugar and whipping cream in a large saucepan. Cook, stirring constantly, over medium heat 2 minutes or until bubbly. Stir in vanilla and apple cider. Cook 10 minutes or until thoroughly heated, stirring often.

A MERRY CHRISTMAS EVE DINNER

CLASSIC EGGNOG

HONEY-ROSEMARY CHERRIES AND BLUE CHEESE CROSTINI

SPICE-RUBBED SMOKED TURKEY BREAST WITH MUSHROOM GRAVY

PECAN CORNBREAD

BUTTERNUT SQUASH CASSEROLE WITH PECAN STREUSEL

CRUMB-TOPPED SPINACH CASSEROLE

CRANBERRY CLEMENTINE RELISH

WHITE CHOCOLATE-PEPPERMINT MOUSSE PIE

CLASSIC EGGNOG

MAKES 9 CUPS • HANDS-ON 35 MIN. • TOTAL 4 HR., 5 MIN.

- 6 cups milk
- 2 cups heavy cream
- 1/8 tsp. ground nutmeg
- 12 pasteurized egg yolks
- 2 cups sugar

Praline or bourbon liqueur (optional)

Freshly ground nutmeg

1. Cook first 3 ingredients in a large saucepan over medium heat, stirring occasionally, 5 to 7 minutes or until steaming or a candy thermometer registers about 150°. Reduce heat to low.

2. Whisk together yolks and sugar in a large saucepan until smooth. Cook over low heat, whisking constantly, until a candy thermometer registers at least 160° (about 25 minutes). Whisk milk mixture into egg mixture. Cool 30 minutes; transfer to a pitcher.

3. Cover and chill 3 to 24 hours. Pour desired amount of praline or bourbon liqueur into each glass, if desired. Top with eggnog. Sprinkle with freshly ground nutmeg.

Honey-Rosemary Cherries and Blue Cheese Crostini

MAKES 8 APPETIZER SERVINGS • HANDS-ON 20 MIN. • TOTAL 30 MIN.

Begin your party casually by offering this appetizer "help-yourself" style. Or, make up single-serving plates and present as a first course at the table.

1   shallot, thinly sliced
2   tsp. olive oil
1   (12-oz.) package frozen dark, sweet pitted cherries, thawed
2   Tbsp. balsamic vinegar
2   Tbsp. honey
¼   tsp. chopped fresh rosemary
⅛   tsp. table salt
⅛   tsp. freshly ground black pepper
2   cups loosely packed arugula
16 (¼-inch-thick) ciabatta bread slices, toasted
1   (8-oz.) wedge blue cheese, thinly sliced*
Garnishes: freshly ground black pepper, fresh rosemary

1. Sauté shallot in hot oil in a medium skillet over medium-high heat 2 to 3 minutes or until tender. Add cherries (and any liquid in package) and next 5 ingredients. Cook, stirring occasionally, 8 to 10 minutes or until thickened. Let stand 10 minutes.

2. Divide arugula among toasted bread slices. Top each with cherry mixture and 1 blue cheese slice.

Manchego or goat cheese may be substituted.

Spice-Rubbed Smoked Turkey Breast with Mushroom Gravy

MAKES 8 SERVINGS • HANDS-ON 25 MIN. • TOTAL 6 HR., 51 MIN., INCLUDING GRAVY

Hickory wood chunks
2   Tbsp. mayonnaise
2   Tbsp. Creole mustard
1   tsp. Worcestershire sauce
5-   to 6-lb. bone-in turkey breast
2   Tbsp. brown sugar
1½   tsp. paprika
1   tsp. kosher salt
¾   tsp. garlic powder
½   tsp. celery salt
½   tsp. ground cumin
½   tsp. freshly ground black pepper
¼   tsp. onion powder
3   Tbsp. butter, melted
¼   cup apple butter
1   Tbsp. honey
Mushroom Gravy

1. Soak wood chunks in water 30 minutes. Prepare smoker according to manufacturer's directions, bringing internal temperature to 225° to 250°; maintain temperature for 15 to 20 minutes. Drain wood chunks, and place on coals. Add water to pan to depth of fill line.

2. Combine mayonnaise and next 2 ingredients; rub evenly over turkey breast. Combine brown sugar and next 7 ingredients; sprinkle evenly over turkey, pressing to adhere.

4. Place turkey on upper cooking grate; cover with smoker lid. Smoke for 3½ hours, maintaining temperature inside smoker between 225° and 250°.

5. Stir together butter, apple butter, and honey. Baste turkey with half of butter mixture.

6. Cover and cook 1½ more hours or until a meat thermometer inserted in thickest portion registers 165°, basting with remaining butter mixture during last 30 minutes. Remove turkey from smoker, and let stand 15 minutes before slicing. Serve with Mushroom Gravy.

MUSHROOM GRAVY

MAKES 10 TO 12 SERVINGS · HANDS-ON 26 MIN. · TOTAL 26 MIN.

2	Tbsp. butter
1	(8-oz.) package sliced baby portobello mushrooms
¼	cup dry sherry
2	Tbsp. all-purpose flour
2	cups vegetable broth
½	cup whipping cream
2	tsp. chopped fresh thyme
½	tsp. table salt
½	tsp. freshly ground black pepper

1. Melt butter in a large skillet over medium-high heat. Add mushrooms; sauté 5 to 6 minutes or until tender. Stir in sherry, and cook 1 minute or until liquid almost evaporates. Stir in flour, and cook, stirring constantly, 1 minute. Gradually stir in broth. Bring to a boil; reduce heat, and simmer, stirring constantly, 5 minutes or until slightly thickened.

2. Stir in cream. Simmer 8 minutes, stirring constantly, or until thickened. Remove from heat, and stir in thyme, salt, and black pepper.

PECAN CORNBREAD

MAKES 6 TO 8 SERVINGS · HANDS-ON 5 MIN. · TOTAL 35 MIN.

Serve this cornbread with pepper jelly and butter.

⅓	cup shortening
2	cups yellow self-rising cornmeal mix
1	Tbsp. sugar
½	tsp. ground red pepper
2	cups buttermilk
1	large egg
1	cup finely chopped toasted pecans

1. Preheat oven to 425°. Melt shortening in a 10-inch cast-iron skillet in oven 5 minutes.

2. Stir together cornmeal mix, sugar, and ground red pepper in a medium bowl. Whisk together buttermilk and egg; add to cornmeal mixture, stirring just until moistened. Stir in pecans.

3. Remove skillet from oven; tilt skillet to coat, and pour shortening into batter, stirring until blended. Immediately pour batter into hot skillet.

4. Bake at 425° for 25 minutes or until edges are golden brown.

BUTTERNUT SQUASH CASSEROLE WITH PECAN STREUSEL

MAKES 8 TO 10 SERVINGS · HANDS-ON 15 MIN. · TOTAL 1 HR.

As an option, you can use canned pumpkin puree or yams instead of the squash in this recipe.

3	(12-oz.) packages frozen cooked butternut squash, thawed
1	cup firmly packed light brown sugar
½	cup half-and-half
¼	cup butter, melted
2	large eggs, lightly beaten
½	tsp. table salt
½	tsp. ground cinnamon
¼	tsp. ground allspice
¼	tsp. ground cloves
1	tsp. vanilla extract
¼	cup all-purpose flour
¼	cup firmly packed light brown sugar
3	Tbsp. cold butter, cut into pieces
½	cup chopped pecans

1. Preheat oven to 375°. Combine first 10 ingredients in a large bowl; stir well. Spoon into a lightly greased 11 x 7-inch baking dish.

2. Combine flour and ¼ cup brown sugar. Cut in 3 Tbsp. butter with a pastry blender until crumbly. Stir in nuts. Sprinkle over squash.

3. Bake, uncovered, at 375° for 40 minutes or until edges are lightly browned. Let casserole stand 5 minutes before serving.

Note: We tested with McKenzie's frozen butternut squash.

CRUMB-TOPPED SPINACH CASSEROLE

MAKES 8 TO 10 SERVINGS · HANDS-ON 20 MIN. · TOTAL 50 MIN.

This quick, cheesy side, with its crunchy herbed topping, can be ready to bake in just over the time it takes to preheat the oven.

2	Tbsp. butter
1	medium onion, diced
2	garlic cloves, minced
4	(10-oz.) packages frozen chopped spinach, thawed
½	(8-oz.) package cream cheese, softened
2	Tbsp. all-purpose flour
2	large eggs
½	tsp. table salt
¼	tsp. freshly ground black pepper
1	cup milk
1	(8-oz.) package shredded Cheddar cheese
1	cup Italian-seasoned panko (Japanese breadcrumbs) or homemade breadcrumbs
3	Tbsp. butter, melted

1. Preheat oven to 350°. Melt 2 Tbsp. butter in a large nonstick skillet over medium heat. Add onion and garlic, and sauté 8 minutes or until tender.

2. Meanwhile, drain spinach well, pressing between paper towels to remove excess moisture.

3. Combine cream cheese and flour in a large bowl until smooth. Whisk in eggs, salt, and pepper. Gradually whisk in milk until blended. Add sautéed onion mixture, spinach, and Cheddar, stirring to blend. Spoon into a lightly greased 11- x 7-inch baking dish.

4. Combine breadcrumbs and 3 Tbsp. melted butter in a small bowl; toss well, and sprinkle over casserole.

5. Bake, uncovered, at 350° for 30 to 35 minutes or until thoroughly heated and breadcrumbs are browned.

CRANBERRY CLEMENTINE RELISH

MAKES 4 CUPS · HANDS-ON 10 MIN. · TOTAL 8 HR., 10 MIN.

The cranberries in this recipe are left raw and shredded for extra crunch and tartness. Be sure to use clementines which, unlike tangerines, are seedless.

4	clementines
1	Granny Smith apple, peeled, cored, and cut into eighths
1	(12-oz.) package fresh or frozen cranberries, thawed
½	cup sugar
½	cup honey
¼	cup orange liqueur

Garnish: orange rind curl

1. Grate zest from clementines to equal 4 tsp. Peel clementines, and separate into segments.

2. Process zest, clementine segments, apple, and cranberries in a food processor until chopped. Transfer fruit to a bowl. Stir in sugar and remaining 2 ingredients.

3. Cover and chill 8 hours or overnight. Serve with a slotted spoon.

White Chocolate-Peppermint Mousse Pie

MAKES 8 TO 10 SERVINGS · HANDS-ON 30 MIN. · TOTAL 8 HR., 40 MIN.

This do-ahead frozen dessert makes a perfect ending to a holiday meal.

24 cream-filled chocolate sandwich cookies, finely crushed

6 Tbsp. butter, melted

2 (4-oz.) white chocolate baking bars, chopped

3 Tbsp. whipping cream

½ tsp. peppermint extract or 2 tsp. peppermint liqueur

3 large egg whites

¾ cup sugar

12 drops red liquid food coloring

1½ cups whipping cream, whipped

Garnishes: frozen whipped topping, thawed; coarsely crushed hard peppermint candies; white chocolate shavings

1. Stir together chocolate crumbs and melted butter; press firmly into an ungreased 9-inch deep-dish pie plate.

2. Microwave white chocolate in a microwave-safe bowl at HIGH 1 minute, stirring after 30 seconds. Microwave 3 Tbsp. whipping cream in a glass measuring cup at HIGH 30 seconds. Pour hot cream over white chocolate; let stand 1 minute. Stir until smooth. Stir in peppermint extract; cool 10 minutes.

3. Pour water to depth of 1 inch into bottom of a double boiler over medium heat; bring to a boil. Reduce heat, and simmer; place egg whites and sugar in top of double boiler over simmering water. Cook, whisking constantly, 3 minutes or until sugar is dissolved. Beat egg white mixture over simmering water at medium speed with a handheld mixer until soft peaks form. Add food coloring. Increase speed to high, and beat until stiff peaks form. Fold in white chocolate mixture. Fold in whipped cream.

4. Spoon mousse mixture into prepared pie plate; cover and freeze 8 to 12 hours.

CHRISTMAS MORNING BRUNCH

WINTER CITRUS MOCKTAIL

CINNAMON COFFEE WITH
BOURBON CREAM

HUMMINGBIRD PANCAKES

ITALIAN CREAM PANCAKES

CARROT CAKE PANCAKES

RED VELVET PANCAKES

GERMAN CHOCOLATE PANCAKES

CARAMEL CAKE PANCAKES

WINTER CITRUS MOCKTAIL

MAKES 6 SERVINGS • HANDS-ON 16 MIN. • TOTAL 1 HR., 16 MIN.

This refreshing mocktail is made with one of winter's prized fruits: the blood orange. The tart-sweet flavor of its scarlet-hued flesh—combined with thyme-infused simple syrup and aromatic bitters, then topped off with sparkling water—makes a delicious and refreshing nonalcoholic beverage with a pleasantly bitter undertone.

1   cup sugar
6   thyme sprigs
Ice cubes
3   cups fresh or refrigerated blood orange juice
1½   tsp. aromatic bitters
2   cups lemon-flavored sparkling water
Garnish: fresh thyme sprigs

1. Bring sugar and 1 cup water to a boil in a medium saucepan over medium-high heat. Boil, stirring often, 1 minute or until sugar is dissolved and mixture is clear. Remove from heat; add thyme sprigs, and cool completely (about 1 hour). Remove and discard thyme.

2. Fill 6 (12-oz.) glasses with ice cubes, filling each three-fourths full. Add 2 Tbsp. thyme simple syrup, ½ cup blood orange juice, ¼ tsp. aromatic bitters, and ⅓ cup sparkling water to each glass; stir. Serve immediately.

CINNAMON COFFEE WITH BOURBON CREAM

MAKES 8 CUPS • HANDS-ON 11 MIN. • TOTAL 21 MIN.

1   cup medium-roast ground coffee
1   tsp. ground cinnamon
1   cup heavy cream
2   Tbsp. light brown sugar
2   Tbsp. bourbon
Additional ground cinnamon
8   (3-inch) cinnamon sticks (optional)

1. Combine ground coffee and 1 tsp. cinnamon in a coffee filter. Brew coffee in a 12-cup coffeemaker according to manufacturer's instructions, using 8 cups water.

2. Meanwhile, beat heavy cream at high speed with an electric mixer until foamy; add brown sugar, 1 Tbsp. at a time, beating until soft peaks form. Stir in bourbon. Chill until ready to serve.

3. Top each serving with bourbon cream, additional ground cinnamon, and, if desired, a cinnamon stick.

Note: Eight cups of water poured into a coffeemaker show as 12 cups in the coffeepot.

HUMMINGBIRD PANCAKES

MAKES ABOUT 18 PANCAKES · HANDS-ON 30 MIN. · TOTAL 45 MIN., INCLUDING ANGLAISE

1½	cups all-purpose flour
2	tsp. baking powder
¾	tsp. table salt
½	tsp. ground cinnamon
1½	cups buttermilk
1	cup mashed very ripe bananas
½	cup drained canned crushed pineapple in juice
⅓	cup sugar
1	large egg, lightly beaten
3	Tbsp. canola oil
½	cup chopped toasted pecans

Cream Cheese Anglaise

Garnishes: sliced bananas, chopped fresh pineapple

1. Stir together first 4 ingredients in a large bowl. Whisk together buttermilk and next 5 ingredients in another bowl. Gradually stir buttermilk mixture into flour mixture just until dry ingredients are moistened. Fold in toasted pecans.

2. Pour about ¼ cup batter for each pancake onto a hot, buttered griddle or large nonstick skillet. Cook 3 to 4 minutes or until tops are covered with bubbles and edges look dry and cooked. Turn and cook 3 to 4 minutes or until done. Place in a single layer on a baking sheet, and keep warm in a 200° oven up to 30 minutes. Serve with Cream Cheese Anglaise.

Note: When using a griddle, heat it to 350°.
Tip: For tender pancakes, don't overmix the batter; it should be lumpy.

CREAM CHEESE ANGLAISE

MAKES ABOUT 1¾ CUPS · HANDS-ON 15 MIN. · TOTAL 15 MIN.

1½	cups half-and-half
½	(8-oz.) package cream cheese, softened
⅓	cup sugar
3	large egg yolks
1	Tbsp. cornstarch
⅛	tsp. table salt
2	Tbsp. butter
1	tsp. vanilla extract

1. Process first 6 ingredients in a blender until smooth. Bring mixture to a boil in a medium saucepan over medium heat, whisking constantly. Boil, whisking constantly, 1 minute. Remove from heat, and whisk in butter and vanilla. Serve immediately.

ITALIAN CREAM PANCAKES

MAKES ABOUT 18 PANCAKES • HANDS-ON 35 MIN. • TOTAL 50 MIN., INCLUDING SYRUP

2/3 cup finely chopped pecans

1/2 cup sweetened flaked coconut

2 cups all-purpose flour

1/3 cup sugar

1 tsp. baking powder

1/2 tsp. baking soda

1/2 tsp. table salt

1 cup buttermilk

3/4 cup heavy cream

2 Tbsp. butter, melted

2 tsp. vanilla extract

2 large eggs, separated

Cream Cheese Syrup

Garnish: chopped toasted pecans

1. Preheat oven to 350°. Bake pecans and coconut in a single layer in a shallow pan 5 to 7 minutes or until lightly toasted and fragrant, stirring halfway through.

2. Stir together flour and next 4 ingredients in a large bowl. Whisk together buttermilk, next 3 ingredients, and egg yolks in another bowl. Gradually stir buttermilk mixture into flour mixture just until dry ingredients are moistened. Stir in toasted pecans and coconut. Beat egg whites at high speed with an electric mixer until stiff peaks form; fold into batter.

3. Pour about 1/4 cup batter for each pancake onto a hot, buttered griddle or large nonstick skillet. Cook 3 to 4 minutes or until tops are covered with bubbles and edges look dry and cooked. Turn and cook 3 to 4 minutes or until done. Place in a single layer on a baking sheet, and keep warm in a 200° oven up to 30 minutes. Serve with Cream Cheese Syrup.

Note: When using a griddle, heat it to 350°.

CREAM CHEESE SYRUP

MAKES ABOUT 1¼ CUPS • HANDS-ON 10 MIN. • TOTAL 10 MIN.

1/2 (8-oz.) package cream cheese, softened

1/4 cup butter, softened

1/4 cup maple syrup

1 tsp. vanilla extract

1 cup powdered sugar

1/4 cup milk

1. Beat first 4 ingredients at medium speed with an electric mixer until creamy. Gradually add powdered sugar, beating until smooth. Gradually add milk, beating until smooth. If desired, microwave in a microwave-safe bowl at HIGH 10 to 15 seconds or just until warm; stir until smooth.

CARROT CAKE PANCAKES

MAKES ABOUT 24 PANCAKES • HANDS-ON 40 MIN. • TOTAL 50 MIN., INCLUDING CREAM TOPPING

Use the small holes of a box grater to finely grate the carrots by hand; if you use a food processor, the carrots will be too wet, making the pancakes dense and less tender.

1³/4 cups all-purpose flour

1¹/2 tsp. baking powder

1 tsp. baking soda

1 tsp. ground cinnamon

1 tsp. table salt

2 cups buttermilk

1/3 cup firmly packed light brown sugar

1/4 cup butter, melted

2 large eggs, lightly beaten

2 tsp. vanilla extract

2 cups finely grated carrots (about 1 lb.)

1/2 cup chopped toasted pecans

1/3 cup chopped golden raisins

Mascarpone Cream

Garnish: carrot curls

1. Stir together first 5 ingredients in a large bowl. Whisk together buttermilk and next 4 ingredients in another bowl. Gradually stir buttermilk mixture into flour mixture just until dry ingredients are moistened. Fold in carrots and next 2 ingredients.

2. Pour about ¼ cup batter for each pancake onto a hot, buttered griddle or large nonstick skillet. Cook 3 to 4 minutes or until tops are covered with bubbles and edges look dry and cooked. Turn and cook 3 to 4 minutes or until done. Place in a single layer on a baking sheet, and keep warm in a 200° oven up to 30 minutes. Serve with Mascarpone Cream.

Note: When using a griddle, heat it to 350°.

MASCARPONE CREAM
MAKES ABOUT 2½ CUPS • HANDS-ON 10 MIN. • TOTAL 10 MIN.

1   (8-oz.) container mascarpone cheese

¼   cup powdered sugar

2   tsp. vanilla extract

1   cup whipping cream

1. Whisk together first 3 ingredients in a large bowl just until blended. Beat whipping cream at medium speed with an electric mixer until stiff peaks form. Fold whipped cream into mascarpone mixture.

RED VELVET PANCAKES
MAKES 24 PANCAKES • HANDS-ON 35 MIN. • TOTAL 50 MIN., INCLUDING BUTTER

The Loveless Cafe, Nashville's famous down-home spot, is best known for biscuits, but we love its festive pancakes.

2   cups all-purpose flour

1   cup powdered sugar

½   cup unsweetened cocoa

1½   tsp. baking powder

½   tsp. baking soda

½   tsp. table salt

1½   cups buttermilk

2   large eggs

½   cup granulated sugar

2   Tbsp. red liquid food coloring

Sweet Cream-Cheese Butter

Garnish: powdered sugar

1. Sift together first 6 ingredients into a large bowl. Whisk together buttermilk and next 3 ingredients in another bowl. Gradually stir buttermilk mixture into flour mixture just until dry ingredients are moistened.

2. Pour about ¼ cup batter for each pancake onto a hot, buttered griddle or large nonstick skillet. Cook 3 to 4 minutes or until tops are covered with bubbles and edges look dry and cooked. Turn and cook 3 to 4 minutes or until done. Place in a single layer on a baking sheet, and keep warm in a 200° oven up to 30 minutes. Serve with Sweet Cream-Cheese Butter.

Note: When using a griddle, heat it to 350°.

SWEET CREAM-CHEESE BUTTER
MAKES 4 CUPS • HANDS-ON 15 MIN. • TOTAL 15 MIN.

1   (8-oz.) package cream cheese, softened

1   cup butter, softened

3   cups powdered sugar

1   tsp. vanilla extract

1. Beat cream cheese and butter at medium speed with an electric mixer until creamy. Gradually add powdered sugar, beating at low speed until blended after each addition. Add vanilla, beating until blended.

German Chocolate Pancakes

MAKES ABOUT 20 PANCAKES · HANDS-ON 35 MIN. · TOTAL 55 MIN., INCLUDING SYRUP

2   cups all-purpose flour

½   cup sugar

½   cup unsweetened cocoa

1½   Tbsp. baking powder

1   tsp. table salt

2   cups milk

2   large eggs, lightly beaten

½   (4-oz.) sweet chocolate baking bar, finely chopped

3   Tbsp. butter, melted

1   tsp. vanilla extract

German Chocolate Syrup

Garnishes: coconut flakes, chocolate curls

1. Whisk together first 5 ingredients in a large bowl. Whisk together milk and next 4 ingredients in another bowl. Gradually stir milk mixture into flour mixture just until moistened.

2. Pour about ¼ cup batter for each pancake onto a hot, buttered griddle or large nonstick skillet. Cook 3 to 4 minutes or until tops are covered with bubbles and edges look dry and cooked. Turn and cook 3 to 4 minutes or until done. Place in a single layer on a baking sheet, and keep warm in a 200° oven up to 30 minutes. Serve with German Chocolate Syrup.

Note: When using a griddle, heat it to 350°.

German Chocolate Syrup

MAKES 1½ CUPS · HANDS-ON 15 MIN. · TOTAL 20 MIN.

⅔   cup chopped pecans

⅔   cup sweetened flaked coconut

1   (5-oz.) can evaporated milk

½   cup firmly packed light brown sugar

¼   cup butter, melted

2   large egg yolks, lightly beaten

½   tsp. vanilla extract

1. Preheat oven to 350°. Bake pecans and coconut in a single layer in a shallow pan 5 to 7 minutes or until lightly toasted and fragrant, stirring halfway through.

2. Cook evaporated milk and next 3 ingredients in a heavy 2-qt. saucepan over medium heat, stirring constantly, 8 to 10 minutes or until mixture bubbles and begins to thicken. Remove from heat, and stir in vanilla, pecans, and coconut. Serve immediately, or store in an airtight container in refrigerator up to 1 week.

To reheat: Microwave syrup in a microwave-safe bowl at HIGH 10 to 15 seconds or just until warm; stir until smooth.

Caramel Cake Pancakes

MAKES ABOUT 15 PANCAKES · HANDS-ON 30 MIN. · TOTAL
40 MIN., INCLUDING SYRUP

2 cups self-rising flour

½ cup sugar

1 cup milk

2 large eggs

3 Tbsp. butter, melted

2 tsp. vanilla extract

Caramel Syrup

1. Whisk together first 2 ingredients in a large bowl. Whisk together milk and next 3 ingredients in another bowl. Gradually stir milk mixture into flour mixture just until dry ingredients are moistened.

2. Pour about ¼ cup batter for each pancake onto a hot, buttered griddle or large nonstick skillet. Cook 3 to 4 minutes or until tops are covered with bubbles and edges look dry and cooked. Turn and cook 3 to 4 minutes or until done. Place in a single layer on a baking sheet, and keep warm in a 200° oven up to 30 minutes. Serve with Caramel Syrup.

Caramel Syrup

MAKES 1¾ CUPS · HANDS-ON 10 MIN. · TOTAL 10 MIN.

½ cup butter

1 cup sugar

1 tsp. fresh lemon juice

¾ cup whipping cream

1. Melt butter in a heavy saucepan over medium heat; add sugar and lemon juice, and cook, stirring constantly, 5 to 6 minutes or until mixture turns a caramel color. Gradually add whipping cream (mixture will boil vigorously), and cook, stirring constantly, 1 to 2 minutes or until smooth. Serve immediately, or store in an airtight container in refrigerator up to 1 week.

To reheat: Microwave in a microwave-safe bowl at HIGH 10 to 15 seconds or just until warm; stir until smooth.

CHRISTMAS DINNER

RUBY RED NEGRONI

PECAN SOUP

HONEY-CURRY GLAZED LAMB WITH
ROASTED GRAPES AND CRANBERRIES

GREEN BEANS WITH HOLLANDAISE SAUCE

SAVORY BACON-AND-LEEK
BREAD PUDDING

ROASTED BEETS WITH HERBED DIJON
VINAIGRETTE

GINGERSNAP-MEYER LEMON
MERINGUE TART

RUBY RED NEGRONI

MAKES 6 SERVINGS • HANDS-ON 7 MIN. • TOTAL 7 MIN.

Our twist on the classic Negroni features fresh Ruby Red grapefruit juice for a festive drink to ring in the holidays.

2   cups fresh red grapefruit juice (3 large grapefruit)
1   cup gin
1   cup Campari
1   cup sweet vermouth
Crushed ice
1½   cups club soda
Garnish: fresh orange slices

1. Stir together first 4 ingredients in a pitcher. Cover and chill.

2. Fill 6 double old-fashioned glasses with crushed ice. Divide juice mixture evenly among glasses. Top each serving with ¼ cup club soda, and stir gently. Serve immediately.

PECAN SOUP

MAKES 13 CUPS • HANDS-ON 36 MIN. • TOTAL 1 HR., 6 MIN.

This velvety, rich appetizer is like chestnut soup with Southern flair. Ladle it into small cups.

½   cup butter
3   celery ribs, coarsely chopped
2   sweet onions, chopped
1   large baking potato, peeled and coarsely chopped
4   cups chicken broth
3   cups heavy cream
1   tsp. table salt
½   tsp. ground white pepper
1   lb. toasted pecan halves
Garnishes: crème fraîche, chopped chives, additional
      toasted pecan halves

1. Melt butter in a Dutch oven over medium heat; add celery and onion. Sauté 20 minutes or until tender.

2. Add potato and next 5 ingredients. Bring to a boil; reduce heat to medium-low, and simmer, uncovered, 30 minutes or until slightly thickened and potato is very tender. Remove from heat; cool slightly.

3. Process soup mixture, in batches, in a blender until smooth, stopping to scrape down sides as needed. Ladle into serving bowls. Serve hot.

HONEY-CURRY GLAZED LAMB WITH ROASTED GRAPES AND CRANBERRIES

MAKES 6 SERVINGS • HANDS-ON 15 MIN. • TOTAL 1 HR., 30 MIN., INCLUDING GRAPES AND CRANBERRIES

Consider ordering lamb from your butcher a few days ahead.

3	(8-rib) lamb rib roasts (1½ lb. each), trimmed
1	Tbsp. red curry powder
1½	tsp. kosher salt
1½	tsp. freshly ground black pepper
	Roasted Grapes and Cranberries
5	Tbsp. olive oil
2	Tbsp. honey
	Garnish: fresh rosemary sprigs

1. Preheat oven to 425°. Sprinkle lamb on all sides with curry powder, salt, and pepper. Let stand 30 minutes.

2. Meanwhile, prepare Roasted Grapes and Cranberries as directed.

3. Cook lamb in 1 Tbsp. hot oil in a 12-inch cast-iron skillet over medium heat 6 to 7 minutes, turning often to brown tops and sides. Place roasts, meat sides up, in skillet. Stir together honey and remaining 4 Tbsp. olive oil; brush mixture on tops and sides of lamb.

4. Bake at 425° for 15 to 18 minutes or until a meat thermometer inserted into thickest portion registers 135°. Remove lamb from oven; let stand 10 minutes. Cut into chops, and serve with Roasted Grapes and Cranberries.

ROASTED GRAPES AND CRANBERRIES

MAKES 6 SERVINGS • HANDS-ON 5 MIN. • TOTAL 20 MIN.

You can also pair this dish with grilled pork tenderloin or add it to a cheese tray.

6	to 8 seedless green or red grape clusters (about 1 lb.)
1	cup fresh cranberries
1	Tbsp. olive oil
1	tsp. chopped fresh rosemary

1. Preheat oven to 400°. Place grape clusters on a 15- x 10-inch jelly-roll pan. Stir together cranberries, olive oil, and rosemary in a small bowl. Spoon mixture over grape clusters.

2. Bake at 400° for 15 to 18 minutes or until grapes begin to blister and cranberry skins begin to split, shaking pan occasionally. Serve immediately, or let stand up to 4 hours.

Green Beans with Hollandaise Sauce

MAKES 8 SERVINGS · HANDS-ON 15 MIN. · TOTAL 15 MIN.

Tie green beans in small bundles of five or six with chives that have been boiled for five seconds.

- ½ cup butter
- 4 large pasteurized egg yolks
- 2 Tbsp. fresh lemon juice
- ½ tsp. kosher salt
- ⅛ tsp. ground white pepper
- Dash of hot sauce (optional)
- 1 lb. haricots verts (French green beans), blanched or steamed

1. Melt butter in a small saucepan over medium heat; reduce heat to low, and keep warm. Process egg yolks, next 3 ingredients, 1 Tbsp. water, and, if desired, hot sauce in a blender or food processor 2 to 3 minutes or until pale and fluffy. With blender running, add melted butter in a slow, steady stream, processing until smooth. Serve warm with beans.

Savory Bacon-and-Leek Bread Pudding

MAKES 6 TO 8 SERVINGS · HANDS-ON 40 MIN. · TOTAL 1 HR., 20 MIN.

We love how buttery Gouda and nutty Parmesan lend richness and depth of flavor to this dish. Bake it as directed, or divide among six to eight ovenproof dishes, reducing the bake time to 30 minutes.

- 8 large eggs, lightly beaten
- 1 cup half-and-half
- 1 cup heavy cream
- 2 tsp. kosher salt
- 1 tsp. dried thyme
- 1 tsp. dried marjoram
- 1 tsp. freshly ground black pepper
- 6 cups cubed challah bread (about 1-inch cubes)
- 1¼ cups grated Gouda cheese, divided
- 1¼ cups freshly grated Parmesan cheese, divided
- 2 leeks, thinly sliced
- 2 Tbsp. butter
- 2 garlic cloves, minced
- 8 cooked bacon slices, crumbled

1. Preheat oven to 350°. Whisk together first 7 ingredients in a large bowl; stir in bread cubes and 1 cup each Gouda and Parmesan cheeses.

2. Remove and discard root ends and dark green tops of leeks. Cut in half lengthwise, and rinse thoroughly under cold running water to remove grit and sand.

3. Melt butter in a medium skillet over medium heat. Add leeks, and cook, stirring occasionally, 7 to 8 minutes or until tender. Add garlic, and cook, stirring constantly, 1 minute. Fold leek mixture and bacon into egg mixture. Pour into a lightly greased 11- × 7-inch baking dish. Sprinkle with remaining ¼ cup each Gouda and Parmesan cheeses.

4. Bake at 350° for 35 to 40 minutes or until center is set. Let stand 5 minutes.

Roasted Beets with Herbed Dijon Vinaigrette

MAKES 4 TO 6 SERVINGS · HANDS-ON 19 MIN. · TOTAL 49 MIN.

For a colorful presentation, use red and golden beets.

- 3 lb. fresh beets with greens (8 medium)
- 5 Tbsp. olive oil, divided
- 2 Tbsp. chopped fresh flat-leaf parsley
- 2 Tbsp. Dijon mustard
- 1 Tbsp. red wine vinegar
- 2 tsp. chopped fresh rosemary
- 1 tsp. chopped fresh thyme
- 1/4 tsp. table salt
- 1/4 tsp. freshly ground black pepper
- 1/2 cup coarsely chopped toasted pecans

1. Preheat oven to 450°.

2. Trim beet stems to 1 inch. Peel beets, and cut each into 6 wedges. Place beets in a single layer on a 17- x 12-inch half-sheet pan or shallow roasting pan. Drizzle beets with 1 Tbsp. oil. Toss to coat.

3. Roast at 450° for 30 minutes or until beets are tender, turning after 20 minutes.

4. Whisk together remaining 1/4 cup oil, parsley, and next 6 ingredients in a large bowl. Add beets, tossing to coat. Sprinkle with pecans. Serve immediately.

Gingersnap-Meyer Lemon Meringue Tart

MAKES 10 TO 12 SERVINGS · HANDS-ON 25 MIN. · TOTAL 4 HR., 22 MIN.

If Meyer lemons are unavailable, substitute equal amounts of regular lemon juice and orange juice.

Gingersnap Crust
- 2 cups crushed gingersnaps (about 40 gingersnaps)
- 5 Tbsp. butter, melted

Fresh Meyer Lemon Curd
- 1 1/2 cups sugar
- 1/4 cup cornstarch
- 3 large eggs
- 3 large egg yolks
- 2/3 cup fresh Meyer lemon juice
- 1 1/2 Tbsp. Meyer lemon zest
- 1/2 cup cold butter, cut into pieces

Italian Meringue
- 1 cup sugar
- 2 Tbsp. light corn syrup
- 3 large egg whites

Garnish: Meyer lemon slices

1. Prepare Gingersnap Crust: Preheat oven to 350°. Stir together gingersnap crumbs and butter. Firmly press mixture on bottom and up sides of a 10-inch tart pan. Bake at 350° for 9 minutes or until golden and fragrant. Cool in pan on a wire rack 30 minutes.

2. Meanwhile, prepare Fresh Meyer Lemon Curd: Whisk together 1 1/2 cups sugar and cornstarch in a heavy saucepan. Whisk in eggs and egg yolks. Stir in lemon juice. Bring to a boil over medium heat, whisking constantly. Boil, whisking constantly, 1 to 1 1/2 minutes or until thickened. Remove pan from heat. Stir in lemon zest and butter.

3. Fill a large bowl with ice. Place pan containing lemon curd in ice, and let stand, stirring occasionally, 15 minutes. Spread lemon curd over prepared crust. Place heavy-duty plastic wrap directly on lemon curd (to prevent a film from forming); chill 2 hours. (Mixture will thicken as it cools.)

4. Prepare Italian Meringue: Preheat broiler with oven rack 8 inches from heat. Combine 1/4 cup water, 1 cup sugar, and corn syrup in a small heavy saucepan; cook over medium heat, stirring constantly, until clear. Cook, without stirring, until a candy thermometer registers 240° (soft ball stage). Beat egg whites at high speed with an electric mixer until soft peaks form; slowly add syrup mixture, beating constantly. Beat until stiff peaks form. Spoon meringue in center of tart; spread to within 2 inches of edge of tart. Broil 3 to 4 minutes or until golden brown. Cool completely on a wire rack. Chill 1 hour.

CHRISTMAS CAKES

RED VELVET-WHITE CHOCOLATE CHEESECAKE

MAKES 10 TO 12 SERVINGS • HANDS-ON 45 MIN. •
TOTAL 13 HR., 45 MIN.

Whimsy meets elegance in all five layers of this red velvet-white chocolate wonder.

Cheesecake Layers
2   (8-inch) round disposable aluminum foil cake pans
1   (12-oz.) package white chocolate morsels
5   (8-oz.) packages cream cheese, softened
1   cup granulated sugar
2   large eggs
1   Tbsp. vanilla extract

Red Velvet Layers
1   cup butter, softened
2½ cups granulated sugar
6   large eggs
3   cups all-purpose flour
3   Tbsp. unsweetened cocoa
¼   tsp. baking soda
1   (8-oz.) container sour cream
2   tsp. vanilla extract
2   (1-oz.) bottles red liquid food coloring
3   (8-in.) round disposable aluminum foil cake pans

White Chocolate Frosting

2   (4-oz.) white chocolate baking bars, chopped

½   cup boiling water

1   cup butter, softened

1   (32-oz.) package powdered sugar, sifted

⅛   tsp. table salt

Garnishes: store-bought coconut candies, White Candy Leaves

1. Prepare Cheesecake Layers: Preheat oven to 300°. Line bottom and sides of 2 disposable cake pans with aluminum foil, allowing 2 to 3 inches to extend over sides; lightly grease foil.

2. Microwave white chocolate morsels in a microwave-safe bowl according to package directions; cool 10 minutes.

3. Beat cream cheese and melted chocolate at medium speed with an electric mixer until creamy; gradually add 1 cup sugar, beating well. Add 2 eggs, 1 at a time, beating just until yellow disappears after each addition. Stir in 1 Tbsp. vanilla. Pour into prepared pans.

4. Bake at 300° for 30 to 35 minutes or until almost set. Turn oven off. Let cheesecakes stand in oven, with door closed, 30 minutes. Remove from oven to wire racks; cool completely (about 1½ hours). Cover and chill 8 hours, or freeze 24 hours to 2 days.

5. Prepare Red Velvet Layers: Preheat oven to 350°. Beat 1 cup butter at medium speed with a heavy-duty electric stand mixer until creamy. Gradually add 2½ cups sugar, beating until light and fluffy. Add 6 eggs, 1 at a time, beating just until blended after each addition.

6. Stir together flour and next 2 ingredients; add to butter mixture alternately with sour cream, beginning and ending with flour mixture. Beat at low speed just until blended after each addition. Stir in 2 tsp. vanilla; stir in food coloring. Spoon batter into 3 greased and floured 8-inch disposable cake pans.

7. Bake at 350° for 20 to 24 minutes or until a wooden pick inserted in center comes out clean. Cool in pans on wire racks 10 minutes. Remove from pans to wire racks; cool completely (about 1 hour).

8. Prepare White Chocolate Frosting: Whisk together chocolate and ½ cup boiling water until chocolate melts. Cool 20 minutes; chill 30 minutes.

9. Beat 1 cup butter and chilled chocolate mixture at low speed until blended. Beat at medium speed 1 minute. Increase speed to high; beat 2 to 3 minutes or until fluffy. Gradually add powdered sugar and salt, beating at low speed until blended. Increase speed to high; beat 1 to 2 minutes or until smooth and fluffy.

10. Assemble cake: Place 1 layer red velvet on a serving platter. Top with 1 layer cheesecake. Repeat with remaining layers of red velvet and cheesecake, alternating and ending with red velvet on top. Spread top and sides of cake with White Chocolate Frosting. Store in refrigerator.

Tip: Bake the layers in inexpensive disposable cake pans, and start one day ahead to allow the cheesecake layers to chill before assembling.

WHITE CANDY LEAVES

2   oz. vanilla candy coating

1. Select nontoxic leaves, such as bay leaves. Thoroughly wash the leaves, and pat dry. Melt approximately 2 oz. vanilla candy coating in a saucepan over low heat until melted (about 3 minutes). Stir until smooth. Cool slightly. Working on parchment paper, spoon a ⅛-inch-thick layer of candy coating over backs of leaves, spreading to edges.

2. Transfer leaves gently, by their stems, to a clean sheet of parchment paper, resting them candy-coating sides up; let stand until candy coating is firm (about 10 minutes). Gently grasp each leaf at stem end, and carefully peel the leaf away from the candy coating. Store candy leaves in a cold, dry place, such as an airtight container in the freezer, up to 1 week.

3. Handle leaves gently when garnishing, or they'll break or melt. Arrange candy leaves around the base of the cake and store-bought coconut candies (such as Confetteria Raffaello Almond Coconut Treats) in the center of the cake. Accent the top of the cake with additional candy leaves. For candy pearls, simply roll any remaining candy coating into balls, and let stand until dry.

Red Velvet Cake with Coconut-Cream Cheese Frosting

MAKES 10 TO 12 SERVINGS · HANDS-ON 30 MIN. ·
TOTAL 2 HR., 15 MIN.

This cake bakes best in four pans. If you need additional pans, use 8-inch round disposable aluminum foil pans. Just be sure to place them on a baking sheet for stability.

3/4   cup butter, softened
2   cups sugar
3   large eggs
3   Tbsp. red liquid food coloring
1   Tbsp. vanilla extract
2 3/4 cups all-purpose flour
1/2   cup unsweetened cocoa
1   Tbsp. baking powder
3/4   tsp. baking soda
1/4   tsp. table salt
1 1/2 cups buttermilk
      Coconut-Cream Cheese Frosting
      Garnishes: white chocolate trees, fresh cranberries

1. Preheat oven to 350°. Beat butter at medium speed with a heavy-duty electric stand mixer until light and fluffy. Gradually add sugar, beating until blended. Add eggs, 1 at a time, beating until blended after each addition. Add food coloring and vanilla, beating until blended.

2. Whisk together flour and next 4 ingredients; add to butter mixture alternately with buttermilk, beginning and ending with flour mixture. Beat at low speed just until blended after each addition. Spoon batter into 4 greased and floured 8-inch round cake pans.

3. Bake all pans at the same time, with 2 pans on top rack and 2 pans on bottom rack, at 350° for 10 minutes; rotate pans, and bake 10 to 12 more minutes or until a wooden pick inserted in center comes out clean. Cool in pans on wire racks 10 minutes. Remove from pans to wire racks, and cool completely (about 1 hour).

4. Spread about 1 cup Coconut-Cream Cheese Frosting between cake layers; spread remaining frosting on top and sides of cake.

Coconut-Cream Cheese Frosting

MAKES ABOUT 8 CUPS · HANDS-ON 15 MIN. · TOTAL 15 MIN.

2   (8-oz.) packages cream cheese, softened
1   cup butter, softened
1/2   tsp. coconut extract
8   cups powdered sugar
4   cups sweetened shredded coconut

1. Beat cream cheese and butter at medium speed with a heavy-duty electric stand mixer until smooth. Add coconut extract, beating until blended. Gradually add powdered sugar, beating until smooth. Stir in shredded coconut.

Snowy White Layer Cake

MAKES 10 TO 12 SERVINGS · HANDS-ON 40 MIN. · TOTAL 2 HR.

Parchment paper

1 cup milk

1½ tsp. vanilla extract

1 cup butter, softened

2 cups sugar

3 cups cake flour

1 Tbsp. baking powder

5 large egg whites

Vanilla Buttercream Frosting

Garnish: Fondant Snowflakes

1. Preheat oven to 350°. Grease 3 (8-inch) round cake pans; line bottoms with parchment paper, and grease and flour paper.

2. Stir together milk and vanilla.

3. Beat butter at medium speed with a heavy-duty electric stand mixer until creamy; gradually add sugar, beating until light and fluffy. Sift together flour and baking powder; add to butter mixture alternately with milk mixture, beginning and ending with flour mixture. Beat at low speed just until blended after each addition.

4. Beat egg whites at medium speed until stiff peaks form; gently fold into batter. Pour batter into prepared pans.

5. Bake at 350° for 20 to 23 minutes or until a wooden pick inserted in center comes out clean. Cool in pans on wire racks 10 minutes. Remove from pans to wire racks; discard parchment paper. Cool completely (about 40 minutes).

6. Spread Vanilla Buttercream Frosting between layers (about 1 cup per layer) and on top and sides of cake.

Tip: Use a heavy-duty electric stand mixer for best results. Also, lining the bottoms of the pans with parchment paper ensures that the layers come out of the pans with ease.

Vanilla Buttercream Frosting

MAKES 4½ CUPS · HANDS-ON 10 MIN. · TOTAL 10 MIN.

1 cup butter, softened

¼ tsp. table salt

1 (32-oz.) package powdered sugar

6 to 7 Tbsp. milk

1 Tbsp. vanilla extract

1. Beat butter and salt at medium speed with an electric mixer 1 to 2 minutes or until creamy; gradually add powdered sugar alternately with 6 Tbsp. milk, beating at low speed until blended and smooth after each addition. Stir in vanilla. If desired, beat in remaining 1 Tbsp. milk, 1 tsp. at a time, until frosting reaches desired consistency.

Fondant Snowflakes

½ (24-oz.) package white fondant

1 Tbsp. vodka

Edible glitter and sparkling dust

1. Dust work surface with powdered sugar. Roll out fondant to ¼-inch thickness. Cut fondant with various-sized snowflake cutters. Transfer to baking sheets; let dry for 12 hours. To add glimmer, brush snowflakes lightly with vodka. Sprinkle with edible glitter and sparkling dust.

MERRY BERRY CAKE

Prepare Snowy White Layer Cake (page 359) as directed, omitting Vanilla Buttercream Frosting and preparing Merry Berry Filling and White Chocolate Buttercream Frosting. Spread Merry Berry Filling between cake layers, and spread White Chocolate Buttercream Frosting on top and sides of cake. Prepare Almond Bark, and place bark pieces around cake's sides.

MERRY BERRY FILLING

MAKES 2 CUPS · HANDS-ON 15 MIN. · TOTAL 6 HR., 45 MIN.

1   cup fresh cranberries
1   cup fresh raspberries
1/2 cup sugar
2   Tbsp. cornstarch
1   Tbsp. cold water
1   cup chopped fresh strawberries
2   Tbsp. butter

1. Cook first 3 ingredients and 3 Tbsp. water in a medium saucepan over medium-low heat, stirring often, 3 to 4 minutes or until cranberry skins begin to split. Whisk together cornstarch and 1 Tbsp. cold water until smooth; add to cranberry mixture, and cook, stirring constantly, 1 minute. Stir in strawberries and butter until butter is melted. Cool to room temperature (about 30 minutes). Cover and chill 6 hours.

WHITE CHOCOLATE BUTTERCREAM FROSTING

MAKES ABOUT 6 CUPS · HANDS-ON 15 MIN. · TOTAL 45 MIN.

1   (4-oz.) white chocolate baking bar, broken into small pieces
1/3 cup heavy cream
1   cup butter, softened
1   (32-oz.) package powdered sugar
1/4 cup heavy cream
1/8 tsp. kosher salt
2   tsp. vanilla extract

1. Microwave chocolate and 1/3 cup heavy cream in a microwave-safe bowl at MEDIUM (50% power) 1 to 1½ minutes or until melted and smooth, stirring at 30-second intervals. (Do not overheat.) Let cool to room temperature (about 30 minutes).

2. Beat butter at medium speed with an electric mixer until creamy; gradually add powdered sugar and ¼ cup heavy cream, 1 Tbsp. at a time, beating at low speed until blended after each addition. Beat in salt and chocolate mixture until light and fluffy. Stir in vanilla.

ALMOND BARK

1   (24-oz.) package almond bark candy coating, melted
Parchment paper

1. Pour about ³/₄ cup melted candy coating onto parchment paper; spread into a thin 12 x 4-inch rectangle. Transfer parchment to top of a muffin pan; freeze 20 minutes. Repeat 4 times. Let bark stand at room temperature 10 minutes; break into pieces. Attach to cake with frosting, pressing gently to adhere. Mound center with berries.

Bourbon Eggnog Cake

Prepare Snowy White Layer Cake (page 359) as directed, omitting Vanilla Buttercream Frosting and preparing Eggnog Filling and Bourbon-Vanilla Bean Frosting. Spread Eggnog Filling between cake layers, and spread Bourbon-Vanilla Bean Frosting on top and sides of cake. Prepare Fondant Holly. Arrange leaves and fresh cranberries on cake, pressing gently to adhere.

Eggnog Filling

MAKES 2 CUPS • HANDS-ON 15 MIN. • TOTAL 7 HR., 15 MIN.

- 1¾ cups heavy cream
- ⅓ cup sugar
- ¼ cup all-purpose flour
- 2 large eggs
- ¼ tsp. ground nutmeg
- ¼ cup bourbon
- 1 Tbsp. vanilla extract

1. Whisk together first 5 ingredients in a heavy saucepan. Cook over medium-low heat, whisking constantly, 10 to 12 minutes or until mixture reaches a chilled pudding-like thickness. Remove from heat; stir in bourbon and vanilla. Cool to room temperature (about 1 hour). Place plastic wrap directly on mixture (to prevent a film from forming), and chill 6 to 24 hours.

Bourbon-Vanilla Bean Frosting

MAKES 6 CUPS • HANDS-ON 15 MIN. • TOTAL 15 MIN.

- 1 cup butter, softened
- 1 (32-oz.) package powdered sugar
- ½ cup milk
- 5 Tbsp. bourbon
- 2 Tbsp. vanilla bean paste
- ⅛ tsp. table salt

1. Beat butter at medium speed with an electric mixer until creamy; gradually add sugar alternately with milk and bourbon, beating at low speed just until blended after each addition. Stir in vanilla and salt.

Fondant Holly

- ½ (24-oz.) package white fondant

1. Dust work surface with powdered sugar. Roll out fondant to ¼-inch thickness. Cut fondant with a 1¾-inch holly leaf cutter. Draw veins on leaves with a small knife. Crumble 2 sheets of aluminum foil into ropes; arrange on a baking sheet. Drape leaves over foil to curl. Let dry at room temperature 12 hours.

Marbled Pumpkin Praline Cake

MAKES 10 TO 12 SERVINGS · HANDS-ON 50 MIN. · TOTAL 2 HR., 15 MIN.

Pumpkin Batter

Parchment paper

2	cups all-purpose flour
2	tsp. baking soda
2	tsp. ground cinnamon
1/2	tsp. table salt
1/4	tsp. ground nutmeg
1/4	tsp. ground ginger
1/4	tsp. ground cloves
1 1/2	cups granulated sugar
3/4	cup firmly packed light brown sugar
3/4	cup vegetable oil
3	large eggs
1 1/2	cups canned pumpkin
3/4	cup buttermilk

Cream Cheese Batter

2	(3-oz.) packages cream cheese, softened
1/2	cup granulated sugar
6	Tbsp. butter, softened
2	Tbsp. all-purpose flour
1	tsp. vanilla extract
2	large eggs, lightly beaten

Pecan-Praline Filling

1/2	cup firmly packed light brown sugar
1/4	cup butter
1/4	cup corn syrup
1/2	cup half-and-half
2	Tbsp. cornstarch
1	cup chopped toasted pecans
1	tsp. vanilla extract

Spiced Whipped Cream

2	cups heavy cream
6	Tbsp. powdered sugar
3/4	tsp. vanilla extract
1/8	tsp. ground cinnamon

Garnishes: kumquats, sugared pecans, bay leaves

1. Prepare Pumpkin Batter: Preheat oven to 350°. Grease 3 (9-inch) round cake pans. Line bottoms with parchment paper, and grease and flour paper. Combine 2 cups flour and next 6 ingredients in a small bowl. Beat 1 1/2 cups granulated sugar and next 3 ingredients at medium speed with a heavy-duty electric stand mixer until blended. Add pumpkin, beating until blended. Add buttermilk, beating until blended. Gradually add flour mixture, beating at low speed just until blended after each addition. Pour batter into prepared pans.

2. Prepare Cream Cheese Batter: Beat cream cheese and next 4 ingredients at medium speed with a heavy-duty electric stand mixer until creamy. Add eggs, beating until blended. Drop Cream Cheese Batter by heaping tablespoonfuls onto pumpkin batter in pans, and gently swirl with a knife.

3. Bake at 350° for 25 minutes or until a wooden pick inserted in center comes out clean. Cool in pans on wire racks 10 minutes; remove cakes from pans to wire racks, and cool completely (about 40 minutes).

4. Meanwhile, prepare Pecan-Praline Filling: Bring 1/2 cup brown sugar and next 2 ingredients to a boil in a saucepan over medium heat, whisking constantly. Boil, whisking constantly, 1 minute or until sugar is dissolved. Whisk together half-and-half and cornstarch in a small bowl until smooth; gradually add to brown sugar mixture, whisking constantly. Return to a boil, and boil, whisking constantly, 1 minute or until thickened. Stir in pecans and 1 tsp. vanilla. Cool mixture 20 minutes.

5. Spread filling between cooled cake layers.

6. Prepare Spiced Whipped Cream: Beat heavy cream at medium speed with an electric mixer 1 minute. Add powdered sugar and next 2 ingredients, beating until soft peaks form. Spread frosting on top and sides of cake.

Peppermint-Hot Chocolate Cake

MAKES 10 TO 12 SERVINGS · HANDS-ON 40 MIN. · TOTAL 2 HR., 25 MIN.

Full of holiday cheer, this winning cake combines the flavors of a favorite cozy winter drink with the ultimate Christmas candy—fudge.

½ cup boiling water

1 (4-oz.) milk chocolate baking bar, chopped

1 cup butter, softened

2 cups sugar

4 large eggs, separated

1 tsp. vanilla extract

2 cups all-purpose flour

¼ cup unsweetened cocoa

1 tsp. baking soda

1 tsp. table salt

1 cup buttermilk

Fudge Filling

Peppermint-Cream Frosting

1. Preheat oven to 350°. Grease and flour 3 (8-inch) round cake pans.

2. Pour boiling water over chocolate in a heatproof bowl. Stir until chocolate is melted and smooth. Cool to room temperature (about 30 minutes).

3. Beat butter at medium speed with a heavy-duty electric stand mixer until creamy; gradually add sugar, beating until light and fluffy. Add egg yolks, 1 at a time, beating until blended after each addition. Add melted chocolate and vanilla, beating until blended. Combine flour and next 3 ingredients; add to butter mixture alternately with buttermilk, beginning and ending with flour mixture. Beat at low speed just until blended after each addition.

4. Beat egg whites at medium speed until soft peaks form; gently fold into batter. Pour batter into prepared pans.

5. Bake at 350° for 20 to 30 minutes or until a wooden pick inserted in center comes out clean. Cool in pans on wire racks 10 minutes; remove from pans to wire racks, and cool completely (about 40 minutes).

6. Meanwhile, prepare Fudge Filling; spread between cake layers. Spread frosting on top and sides of cake.

Fudge Filling

MAKES 2 CUPS · HANDS-ON 10 MIN. · TOTAL 30 MIN.

1 (14-oz.) can sweetened condensed milk

1 (12-oz.) package semisweet chocolate morsels

¼ tsp. peppermint extract

1. Combine sweetened condensed milk and chocolate morsels in a saucepan, and cook over medium-low heat, stirring constantly, 4 to 6 minutes or until chocolate is melted and smooth. Remove from heat; stir in peppermint extract. Cool filling to room temperature (about 20 minutes).

Peppermint-Cream Frosting

MAKES 3 CUPS · HANDS-ON 5 MIN. · TOTAL 5 MIN.

1 (7-oz.) jar marshmallow crème

1 (8-oz.) container frozen whipped topping, thawed

⅛ tsp. peppermint extract

1. Beat marshmallow crème, whipped topping, and peppermint extract at high speed with an electric mixer 1 to 2 minutes or until glossy, stiff peaks form.

Note: We tested with Nielsen-Massey Pure Peppermint Extract.

Chocolate-Toffee-Gingerbread Cake

MAKES 10 TO 12 SERVINGS · HANDS-ON 45 MIN. ·
TOTAL 3 HR., 5 MIN.

*The addition of hot water at the end of this recipe makes
for an exceptionally moist cake.*

Ginger Whipped Cream (recipe on page 365)

1½	cups semisweet chocolate morsels
1	(16-oz.) package light brown sugar
½	cup butter, softened
3	large eggs
2	cups all-purpose flour
¾	tsp. ground ginger
¾	tsp. ground cinnamon
½	tsp. table salt
½	tsp. ground allspice
¼	tsp. freshly ground nutmeg
1	(8-oz.) container sour cream
1	cup hot water
½	cup molasses
1	tsp. baking soda
2	tsp. vanilla extract

Silky Ganache

1	cup toffee bits

Garnishes: Spiced Sorghum Snowflakes (recipe on
page 338), fresh cranberries, fresh mint

1. Preheat oven to 350°. Prepare Ginger Whipped Cream
as directed in step 1 of recipe (through chilling).

2. Microwave chocolate morsels in a microwave-safe bowl
at HIGH 1 to 1½ minutes or until melted and smooth, stirring at 30-second intervals.

3. Beat brown sugar and butter at medium speed with an
electric mixer until well blended (about 5 minutes). Add
eggs, 1 at a time, beating just until blended after each addition. Add melted chocolate, beating just until blended.

4. Sift together flour and next 5 ingredients. Gradually add
to chocolate mixture alternately with sour cream, beginning
and ending with flour mixture. Beat at low speed just until
blended after each addition. Stir together hot water and
next 2 ingredients. (Mixture will foam.) Gradually stir

molasses mixture and vanilla into chocolate mixture just
until blended. Spoon batter into 3 greased and floured
8-inch round cake pans.

5. Bake at 350° for 25 to 30 minutes or until a wooden
pick inserted in center comes out clean. Cool in pans on
wire racks 10 minutes; remove from pans to wire racks, and
cool completely (about 1 hour).

6. Meanwhile, prepare Silky Ganache. Place 1 cake layer
on a cake stand or serving plate. Spread with half of
ganache; sprinkle with ½ cup toffee bits. Top with second
cake layer; spread with remaining ganache, and sprinkle
with remaining ½ cup toffee bits. Top with remaining cake
layer. Cover and chill 2 to 8 hours.

7. Finish preparing Ginger Whipped Cream as directed in
step 2 of recipe. Spread top and sides of cake with whipped
cream just before serving.

Silky Ganache

MAKES 2¾ CUPS · HANDS-ON 20 MIN. · TOTAL 1 HR., 10 MIN.

For best results, use premium chocolate morsels.

1	(12-oz.) package semisweet chocolate morsels
¼	tsp. table salt
1	(14-oz.) can sweetened condensed milk
2	Tbsp. butter
1	tsp. vanilla extract
2	Tbsp. heavy cream

1. Pour water to depth of 1 inch into bottom of a double
boiler over medium-high heat, and bring to a boil. Reduce
heat to medium-low, and simmer; place chocolate and salt
in top of double boiler over simmering water. Cook, stirring
constantly, 2 to 3 minutes or until melted.

2. Add sweetened condensed milk; cook, stirring constantly, 1 to 2 minutes or until blended and smooth. Remove
from heat; add butter and vanilla, and stir 4 to 5 minutes or
until smooth.

3. Let cool to room temperature (about 45 minutes). Transfer to a bowl. Gradually add cream to chocolate mixture,
and beat at high speed with an electric mixer 2 to 3 minutes
or until smooth and the consistency of a thick buttercream
frosting. Use immediately.

Ginger Whipped Cream

MAKES 4 CUPS • HANDS-ON 15 MIN. • TOTAL 4 HR., 15 MIN.

2   cups heavy cream
5   (1/8-inch-thick) slices peeled fresh ginger
6   Tbsp. powdered sugar

1. Cook cream and ginger in a heavy nonaluminum saucepan over medium-high heat, stirring often, 3 to 5 minutes or just until bubbles appear (do not boil); remove from heat, and let cool completely (about 20 minutes). Chill 4 to 12 hours. (Cream needs to be ice-cold before beating.)

2. Pour cream mixture through a fine wire-mesh strainer into a bowl, discarding ginger. Beat at medium-high speed with an electric mixer 1 minute or until foamy; increase speed to high, and gradually add powdered sugar, beating 2 to 3 minutes or just until stiff peaks form. (Do not overbeat or cream will become grainy.) Use immediately.

Tiramisù Layer Cake

MAKES 10 TO 12 SERVINGS • HANDS-ON 45 MIN. • TOTAL 6 HR., 40 MIN.

1/2   cup butter, softened
1/2   cup shortening
2   cups sugar
2/3   cup milk
3   cups all-purpose flour
1   Tbsp. baking powder
1   tsp. table salt
1   Tbsp. vanilla bean paste*
1   tsp. almond extract
6   large egg whites
Coffee Syrup (recipe on page 366)
Mascarpone Frosting (recipe on page 366)
Garnishes: raspberries, strawberries, red currants, fresh mint

1. Preheat oven to 350°. Beat butter and shortening at medium speed with an electric mixer until fluffy; gradually add sugar, beating well.

2. Stir together milk and 2/3 cup water. Combine flour and next 2 ingredients; add to butter mixture alternately with milk mixture, beginning and ending with flour mixture. Beat at low speed just until blended after each addition. Stir in vanilla bean paste and almond extract.

3. Beat egg whites at high speed until stiff peaks form, and fold into batter. Spoon batter into 3 greased and floured 8-inch round cake pans.

4. Bake at 350° for 25 to 30 minutes or until a wooden pick inserted in center comes out clean. Cool in pans on wire racks 10 minutes; remove from pans to wire racks, and cool completely (about 1 hour).

5. Meanwhile, prepare Coffee Syrup.

6. Prepare Mascarpone Frosting. Pierce cake layers with a wooden pick, making holes 1 inch apart. Brush or spoon Coffee Syrup over layers.

7. Place 1 cake layer, brushed side up, on a cake stand or serving plate. Spread top with 1⅓ cups Mascarpone Frosting. Top with second cake layer, brushed side up, and spread with 1⅓ cups Mascarpone Frosting. Top with remaining cake layer, brushed side up. Spread top and sides of cake with remaining Mascarpone Frosting. Chill 4 hours before serving.

Vanilla extract may be substituted.

Coffee Syrup

MAKES ABOUT 1½ CUPS • HANDS-ON 5 MIN. • TOTAL 1 HR., 5 MIN.

- ½ cup sugar
- ⅔ cup strong brewed coffee
- ¼ cup brandy

1. Combine sugar and ⅓ cup water in a microwave-safe bowl. Microwave at HIGH 1½ minutes or until sugar is dissolved, stirring at 30-second intervals. Stir in coffee and brandy. Cool 1 hour.

Mascarpone Frosting

MAKES ABOUT 8 CUPS • HANDS-ON 20 MIN. • TOTAL 20 MIN.

- 2 (8-oz.) packages mascarpone cheese
- 3 cups heavy cream
- 1 Tbsp. vanilla extract
- ⅔ cup sugar

1. Stir mascarpone cheese in a large bowl just until blended.

2. Beat cream and vanilla at low speed with an electric mixer until foamy; increase speed to medium-high, and gradually add sugar, beating until stiff peaks form. (Do not overbeat or cream will become grainy.) Gently fold whipped cream mixture into mascarpone cheese. Use immediately.

Layered Peppermint Cheesecake

MAKES 10 TO 12 SERVINGS · HANDS-ON 1 HR., 10 MIN. ·
TOTAL 8 HR., 30 MIN.

Peppermint Cheesecake Layers

- 3 (8-oz.) packages cream cheese, softened
- ½ cup sugar
- 2 Tbsp. unsalted butter, softened
- 3 large eggs
- 1 Tbsp. all-purpose flour
- 1½ cups sour cream
- 2 tsp. vanilla extract
- ¼ tsp. peppermint extract
- ⅔ cup crushed hard peppermint candies

Sour Cream Cake Layers

- 1 (18.25-oz.) package white cake mix
- 2 large eggs
- 1 (8-oz.) container sour cream
- ⅓ cup vegetable oil

White Chocolate Mousse Frosting

- ⅔ cup sugar
- 1 cup white chocolate morsels
- 2 cups whipping cream
- 2 tsp. vanilla extract

Garnishes: white chocolate curls, hard peppermint candies

1. Prepare Peppermint Cheesecake Layers: Preheat oven to 325°. Line bottom and sides of 2 (8-inch) round cake pans with aluminum foil, allowing 2 to 3 inches to extend over sides; lightly grease foil. Beat cream cheese, ½ cup sugar, and 2 Tbsp. butter at medium speed with an electric mixer 1 to 2 minutes or until creamy and smooth. Add 3 eggs, 1 at a time, beating until blended after each addition. Add flour and next 3 ingredients, beating until blended. Fold in candies. Pour batter into prepared pans. Place cake pans in a large pan; add water to pan to depth of 1 inch.

2. Bake at 325° for 25 minutes or until set. Remove from oven to wire racks; cool completely in pans (about 1 hour). Cover cheesecakes (do not remove from pans), and freeze 4 to 6 hours or until frozen solid. Lift frozen cheesecakes

from pans, using foil sides as handles. Gently remove foil from cheesecakes. Wrap in plastic wrap, and return to freezer until ready to assemble cake.

3. Prepare Sour Cream Cake Layers: Preheat oven to 350°. Beat cake mix, next 3 ingredients, and ½ cup water at low speed with an electric mixer 30 seconds or just until moistened; beat at medium speed 2 minutes. Spoon batter into 3 greased and floured 8-inch round cake pans.

4. Bake at 350° for 15 to 20 minutes or until a wooden pick inserted in center comes out clean. Cool in pans on wire racks 10 minutes; remove from pans to wire racks, and cool completely (about 1 hour).

5. Prepare White Chocolate Mousse Frosting: Cook ⅔ cup sugar and ¼ cup water in a small saucepan over medium-low heat, stirring often, 3 to 4 minutes or until sugar is dissolved. Add white chocolate morsels; cook, stirring constantly, 2 to 3 minutes or until chocolate is melted and smooth. Remove from heat. Cool to room temperature (about 30 minutes), whisking occasionally.

6. Beat cream and 2 tsp. vanilla at high speed with an electric mixer 1 to 2 minutes or until soft peaks form. Gradually fold white chocolate mixture into whipped cream mixture, folding until mixture reaches spreading consistency.

7. Assemble cake: Place 1 cake layer on a cake stand or plate. Top with 1 frozen cheesecake layer. Top with second cake layer and remaining cheesecake layer. Top with remaining cake layer. Spread top and sides of cake with frosting. Chill until ready to serve.

Gilded Bourbon-Chocolate Cake

MAKES ABOUT 80 SERVINGS · HANDS-ON 6 HR. · TOTAL 1 DAY

2   recipes Sour Cream Chocolate Cake Batter, divided
1   recipe Bourbon Buttercream
4   (¼-inch-thick) wooden cake dowels
1   recipe Dark Chocolate Ganache
1   (9-inch) round cake board
1   (8-inch) round cake board
1   recipe Gilded Bourbon Balls

1. Preheat oven to 325°. Prepare 1 recipe Sour Cream Chocolate Cake Batter, and pour 2 cups batter into 1 greased and floured 6-inch round cake pan and 6 cups batter into 1 greased and floured 9-inch round cake pan.

2. Bake 6-inch cake at 325° for 35 to 40 minutes and 9-inch cake at 325° for 40 minutes or until a wooden pick inserted in center comes out clean. Cool in pans on wire racks 20 minutes. Turn out onto wire racks, and let cool completely (may wrap in plastic wrap and freeze up to 1 month, if desired). Repeat procedure for second 6-inch and 9-inch layers, using second recipe of Sour Cream Chocolate Cake Batter.

3. Cut domed tops off all cake layers, if necessary, using a serrated knife.

4. Place 1 (9-inch) cake layer on a 9-inch round cake board, and place on a cake turner. Top with 1¼ cups Bourbon Buttercream, leaving a ½-inch border. Top with remaining 9-inch layer.

5. Cut 4 wooden dowels to height of 9-inch tier; insert vertically into cake tier about 3 inches from the corner edge, making a square pattern.

6. Spread top and sides of 9-inch tier with 2½ cups Dark Chocolate Ganache; let stand until set.

7. Transfer 9-inch tier to cake stand.

8. Repeat steps 5 and 6 with 2 (6-inch) layers, placing on an 8-inch round cake board and using ¾ cup Bourbon Buttercream between layers; omit dowels.

9. Position 6-inch tier in center of 9-inch tier, smoothing icing to blend tiers, if necessary.

10. Decorate cake with Gilded Bourbon Balls as desired.

Sour Cream Chocolate Cake Batter

MAKES 8 CUPS • HANDS-ON 35 MIN. • TOTAL 35 MIN.

- 1 cup butter, softened
- 2 cups granulated sugar
- 1 cup firmly packed brown sugar
- 6 large eggs
- 2½ cups all-purpose flour
- ¼ tsp. baking soda
- ½ cup unsweetened cocoa
- 1 (8-oz.) container sour cream
- 2 tsp. vanilla extract

1. Beat butter at medium speed with a heavy-duty electric stand mixer 2 minutes or until fluffy. Gradually add sugars, beating at medium speed until blended. Add eggs, 1 at a time, beating just until yellow disappears.

2. Whisk together flour, baking soda, and cocoa. Add to butter mixture alternately with sour cream, beginning and ending with flour mixture, beating at low speed just until blended after each addition. Stir in vanilla.

Gilded Bourbon Balls

MAKES 25 BALLS • HANDS-ON 35 MIN. • TOTAL 16 HR., 35 MIN.

- 1 (16-oz.) package powdered sugar
- ⅓ cup bourbon
- ¼ cup butter, softened
- ⅔ cup chopped toasted pecans
- 1 (12-oz.) package semisweet chocolate morsels
- 1 Tbsp. shortening
- Wax paper
- 1 (150-mg.) box gold leaf petals

1. Stir together first 4 ingredients until blended. Cover and chill 8 hours. Shape mixture into 1-inch balls, squeezing in palm of hand until mixture adheres. Chill 8 hours.

2. Melt chocolate and shortening in a microwave-safe bowl at HIGH for 30 seconds; stir and microwave at HIGH 30 more seconds or just until melted and smooth.

3. Dip bourbon balls in chocolate, and place on wax paper; place 1 gold leaf petal on top using tweezers, and let dry.

Note: We used Paolo Angeletti Gold Petals, available at www.fancyflowers.com.

Bourbon Buttercream

MAKES ABOUT 4½ CUPS • HANDS-ON 10 MIN. • TOTAL 10 MIN.

This is a slightly thicker buttercream, which is important in a tall, tiered cake.

- 1 cup butter, softened
- 1 (32-oz.) package powdered sugar
- ½ cup bourbon
- 2 Tbsp. milk
- 2 tsp. vanilla extract

1. Beat butter at medium speed with an electric mixer until creamy; gradually add powdered sugar alternately with bourbon and milk, beating at low speed until blended after each addition. Stir in vanilla.

Dark Chocolate Ganache

MAKES 4 CUPS • HANDS-ON 15 MIN. • TOTAL 15 MIN.

- 2 (12-oz.) packages dark chocolate morsels
- 1 cup whipping cream
- 6 Tbsp. butter

1. Microwave chocolate and whipping cream in a large microwave-safe bowl at HIGH for 30 seconds. Whisk and microwave at HIGH for 45 seconds or until chocolate begins to melt.

2. Whisk in butter; let stand 10 minutes. Whisk until mixture begins to thicken. Use immediately.

NEW YEAR'S EVE AT THE LAKE

SPIKED SATSUMA CHAMPAGNE

SOUTHERN 75

LEMONY FETA DIP WITH
OVEN-ROASTED TOMATOES

BACON-WRAPPED BOURBON FIGS

PICKLED SHRIMP

PARMESAN-CRUSTED CRAB CAKE BITES
WITH CHIVE AÏOLI

GRITS CROSTINI

ASPARAGUS WITH CURRY DIP

RASPBERRY PANNA COTTA

GERMAN CHOCOLATE CAKE
TRUFFLES

TINY CARAMEL TARTS

SPIKED SATSUMA CHAMPAGNE

MAKES 9½ CUPS · HANDS-ON 13 MIN. · TOTAL 43 MIN.

Frozen orange slices serve double duty as ice cubes and garnish in this bubbly elixir.

    2   satsumas, thinly sliced*
    Wax paper
    ½   cup sugar
    2   cups fresh satsuma orange juice* (about
         9 satsumas)
    ½   cup orange liqueur
    2   (750-milliliter) bottles chilled dry Champagne

1. Arrange orange slices on a baking sheet lined with wax paper; freeze 30 minutes.

2. Meanwhile, combine ½ cup water and sugar in a 2-cup glass measuring cup. Microwave at HIGH 1 minute or until very hot. Stir until sugar dissolves.

3. Combine sugar syrup, juice, and liqueur in a pitcher; chill until ready to serve.

4. Place 1 frozen orange slice in each Champagne glass. Pour ¼ cup juice mixture into each glass. Top with Champagne, and serve immediately.

Fresh tangerines and bottled juice may be substituted. Look for both in the produce section.

SOUTHERN 75

MAKES 3½ CUPS · HANDS-ON 5 MIN. · TOTAL 3 HR., 5 MIN.

    1   cup bourbon
    ½   cup lemon juice
    ⅓   cup powdered sugar
    2   cups chilled hard cider
    Garnishes: apple slices, lemon twists, rosemary sprigs

1. Stir together bourbon, lemon juice, and powdered sugar in a pitcher until sugar dissolves (about 30 seconds). Cover and chill 3 hours and up to 24 hours. Divide among 8 Champagne flutes; top each with ¼ cup chilled hard cider.

Note: We tested with Angry Orchard hard cider.

Lemony Feta Dip with Oven-Roasted Tomatoes

MAKES 8 SERVINGS · HANDS-ON 15 MIN. · TOTAL 45 MIN.

All your favorite flavors of a Greek salad—in a dip! It's a great way to present Mediterranean flavors.

4   plum tomatoes, halved lengthwise and seeded

¼   cup extra virgin olive oil, divided

¼   tsp. table salt

½   tsp. freshly ground black pepper, divided

3   garlic cloves

3   (4-oz.) containers crumbled feta cheese

1   tsp. lemon zest

1½ Tbsp. lemon juice

2   Tbsp. chopped fresh oregano

Pita wedges or pita chips

Garnishes: additional extra virgin olive oil, fresh oregano leaves, chopped kalamata olives

1. Preheat oven to 450°. Place tomato halves, cut sides up, on a jelly-roll pan. Drizzle with 2 Tbsp. olive oil, and sprinkle with salt and ¼ tsp. pepper.

2. Bake at 450° for 30 minutes or until tomato halves are tender and caramelized. Remove tomato halves from oven, cool, and cut into bite-sized pieces.

3. With processor running, drop garlic through food chute; process until minced. Add cheese, lemon zest, lemon juice, chopped oregano, remaining 2 Tbsp. oil, and remaining ¼ tsp. pepper. Process until smooth. Spoon dip into a bowl. Top with tomato. Serve with pita wedges or chips.

Tip: If making dip ahead of time, top with tomato just before serving.

Bacon-Wrapped Bourbon Figs

MAKES 2 DOZEN · HANDS-ON 20 MIN. · TOTAL 41 MIN.

The size of the figs will determine the amount of cheese you'll need.

12   dried Calimyrna figs

¼   cup bourbon

1   (2- to 4-oz.) wedge Gorgonzola cheese, cut into 24 pieces

24 toasted pecan halves

12 fully cooked bacon slices, cut in half crosswise

Wooden picks

1. Combine first 2 ingredients and 1½ cups water in a medium saucepan. Cover and cook over low heat 15 to 20 minutes or until figs are plump and softened. Remove from heat; cool slightly (about 15 minutes). Drain figs; gently pat dry with paper towels.

2. Preheat oven to 350°. Cut figs in half lengthwise. Place 1 cheese piece and 1 pecan half on cut side of each fig half. Wrap 1 bacon piece around each fig, and secure with a wooden pick. Place on a wire rack in a 15- x 10-inch jelly-roll pan.

3. Bake at 350° for 6 to 8 minutes or until bacon is crisp and browned.

Note: We tested with Oscar Mayer Fully Cooked Bacon.

PICKLED SHRIMP

MAKES 12 SERVINGS • HANDS-ON 20 MIN. • TOTAL 8 HR., 20 MIN.

Use decorative picks to serve these well-seasoned, piquant shrimp.

2	lb. unpeeled, large raw shrimp
3	large garlic cloves, sliced
3	bay leaves
2	large lemons, thinly sliced
1	small red onion, thinly sliced
½	cup olive oil
¼	cup white wine vinegar
2	Tbsp. Old Bay seasoning
2	Tbsp. drained capers
1	Tbsp. whole black peppercorns
1	Tbsp. Worcestershire sauce
1	Tbsp. hot sauce
2	tsp. kosher salt
1	tsp. sugar
½	tsp. dried crushed red pepper
¼	cup chopped fresh parsley

1. Peel shrimp; devein, if desired. Cook shrimp in boiling water to cover 3 to 5 minutes or just until shrimp turn pink; drain. Rinse with cold water.

2. Combine shrimp and next 4 ingredients in a large bowl. Whisk together oil and next 9 ingredients; pour over shrimp mixture. Cover and chill 8 hours, stirring occasionally. Remove and discard bay leaves. Stir in parsley just before serving.

PARMESAN-CRUSTED CRAB CAKE BITES WITH CHIVE AÏOLI

MAKES 12 SERVINGS • HANDS-ON 18 MIN. • TOTAL 48 MIN.

These miniature crab cakes are baked rather than pan-fried and are easy to prepare for a crowd. Use a 1-inch scoop to portion the crab mixture evenly among the mini muffin cups. The crab mixture can be made a day in advance. Cover and store in the refrigerator.

6	oz. fresh lump crabmeat, drained
2	(3-oz.) packages cream cheese, softened
⅔	cup grated Parmesan cheese, divided
3	Tbsp. mayonnaise
2	tsp. Dijon mustard
1	tsp. Worcestershire sauce
¾	tsp. Old Bay seasoning
½	tsp. lemon zest
1	large egg yolk
1½	Tbsp. chopped fresh parsley
1¼	cups panko (Japanese breadcrumbs)
¼	cup butter, melted
	Chive Aïoli

1. Preheat oven to 350°. Generously grease 2 (12-cup) miniature muffin pans. Pick crabmeat, removing any bits of shell.

2. Stir cream cheese in a large bowl until smooth. Add ⅓ cup Parmesan cheese and next 6 ingredients; stir until smooth. Fold in crabmeat and parsley.

3. Combine remaining ⅓ cup Parmesan cheese, panko, and melted butter in a medium bowl; toss with a fork until panko is moistened. Spoon 1 Tbsp. panko mixture into each muffin cup; press into bottom and up sides to form crust. Spoon 1 Tbsp. crab mixture into each crust.

4. Bake at 350° for 25 minutes or until golden brown. Cool in pans 5 minutes. Run a knife around edges of crab cakes to loosen; gently lift cakes from pan. Serve warm or at room temperature topped with Chive Aïoli.

Chive Aïoli

MAKES ½ CUP • HANDS-ON 4 MIN. • TOTAL 4 MIN.

Prepare this aïoli up to one day in advance; cover and chill.

½ cup mayonnaise
1 Tbsp. chopped fresh chives
1 tsp. Dijon mustard
1 garlic clove, pressed

1. Combine all ingredients in a small bowl. Cover and chill.

Grits Crostini

MAKES ABOUT 5 DOZEN • HANDS-ON 15 MIN. • TOTAL 1 HR., 30 MIN., INCLUDING APPLES AND ONIONS

1 cup all-purpose flour
4 tsp. baking powder
1 Tbsp. sugar
¼ tsp. table salt
1 cup milk
¼ cup butter, melted
2 large eggs, beaten
1½ cups cooked grits, cooled
Caramelized Apples and Onions
1 cup (4 oz.) shredded fontina cheese
2 Tbsp. minced fresh thyme

1. Preheat oven to 425°. Sift together first 4 ingredients into a bowl. Whisk together milk and next 2 ingredients in another bowl; add to flour mixture, stirring just until moistened. Whisk in grits. Spoon into greased 12-cup muffin pans (1 Tbsp. per cup).

2. Bake, in batches, at 425° for 12 to 15 minutes or until crostini are golden. Immediately remove from pans to wire racks; cool 30 minutes. Reduce oven to 375°.

3. Meanwhile, prepare Caramelized Apples and Onions.

4. Place crostini on a baking sheet. Top each with 1 tsp. Caramelized Apples and Onions; sprinkle with cheese. Bake at 375° for 8 minutes or until cheese is melted. Sprinkle with thyme; serve immediately.

Caramelized Apples and Onions

Melt 3 Tbsp. butter in a large skillet over medium-high heat; add 4 cups diced sweet onions, and sauté 10 minutes or until golden. Stir in 2 cups diced Granny Smith apples; sauté 10 minutes or until caramel colored. Remove from heat; stir in ¼ tsp. each table salt and freshly ground black pepper. Makes 2¾ cups.

Asparagus with Curry Dip

MAKES 2¼ CUPS • HANDS-ON 15 MIN. • TOTAL 20 MIN.

3 to 4 lb. fresh asparagus
2 cups mayonnaise
1 Tbsp. curry powder
2 Tbsp. mustard-mayonnaise sauce
2 Tbsp. ketchup
1 Tbsp. prepared horseradish
1 Tbsp. Worcestershire sauce
2 tsp. grated onion
1 tsp. celery seeds
1 tsp. hot sauce
1 garlic clove, pressed

1. Snap off and discard tough ends of asparagus; arrange asparagus in a steamer basket over boiling water. Cover and steam 6 to 8 minutes or until crisp-tender. Plunge into ice water to stop the cooking process; drain.

2. Stir together mayonnaise and next 9 ingredients. Season to taste with salt. Serve with steamed asparagus.

Note: We tested with Durkee Famous Sauce.

RASPBERRY PANNA COTTA

MAKES 8 SERVINGS • HANDS-ON 20 MIN. • TOTAL 2 HR., 25 MIN.

Cardamom gives this silky custard its holiday flavor.
Use any berry you wish, adjusting the sugar in the mixture
to taste.

1	envelope unflavored gelatin
2	cups cold milk
2	pt. fresh raspberries
3	Tbsp. sugar
2	Tbsp. fresh lemon juice
1	tsp. ground cardamom (optional)
1/3	cup sugar
1	Tbsp. vanilla extract
1/4	tsp. table salt
1 1/2	cups heavy cream

Garnishes: fresh rosemary sprigs, fresh raspberries

1. Sprinkle gelatin over milk in a saucepan; let stand
5 minutes.

2. Meanwhile, place 3 raspberries in each of 8 (6-oz.)
parfait glasses or jars. Mash together 3 Tbsp. sugar, lemon
juice, remaining raspberries, and, if desired, cardamom in
a medium bowl. Spoon 1 Tbsp. mashed raspberry mixture
into each parfait glass. Reserve remaining berry mixture.

3. Stir 1/3 cup sugar, vanilla, and salt into milk mixture in
saucepan, and cook over low heat, stirring constantly,
3 minutes or until sugar dissolves and milk begins to steam.
Remove from heat; stir in cream. Pour milk mixture over
raspberries in parfait glasses (about 1/2 cup per glass).
Chill 2 hours or until firm. Top parfaits with reserved
mashed raspberry mixture just before serving.

GERMAN CHOCOLATE CAKE TRUFFLES

MAKES 8 1/2 DOZEN TRUFFLES • HANDS-ON 58 MIN. • TOTAL 2 HR.,
58 MIN.

Whether you call these truffles or cake balls, they're easy
to make and fun to dip.

1	(18.25-oz.) package German chocolate cake mix
1	(16-oz.) container milk chocolate ready-to-spread frosting
2	cups toasted coconut, divided
1 3/4	cups toasted finely chopped pecans, divided
	Wax paper
4	(7-oz.) containers milk chocolate dipping chocolate
	Candy dipping fork
	Paper or aluminum foil baking cups

1. Prepare cake mix according to package directions in a
lightly greased 13- x 9-inch pan. Let cool completely in pan
(about 30 minutes).

2. Crumble cake into a large bowl. Scoop frosting by
spoonfuls over cake crumbs. Sprinkle with 1 cup each
coconut and pecans; stir gently just until thoroughly
blended. Using a cookie scoop, scoop cake mixture into
1 1/4-inch balls; roll in hands, and place balls on wax paper-
lined baking sheets. Cover and chill 1 hour.

3. Meanwhile, combine remaining 1 cup coconut and
3/4 cup pecans; stir well. Melt dipping chocolate, 1 container
at a time, according to package directions; dip chilled balls
in melted chocolate, using candy dipping fork and allowing
excess chocolate to drip off. Place coated truffles on wax
paper-lined baking sheets. Sprinkle tops with coconut-
pecan mixture; chill 30 minutes or until set. Place truffles
in baking cups.

Note: We tested with Duncan Hines German Chocolate Cake Mix,
Betty Crocker Frosting, and Baker's Real Milk Chocolate Dipping
Chocolate.

TINY CARAMEL TARTS

MAKES 6 DOZEN • HANDS-ON 30 MIN. • TOTAL 4 HR., 30 MIN., INCLUDING PASTRY SHELLS

Add a festive touch! Just before serving, sprinkle tarts with finely chopped chocolate, crystallized ginger, toffee, sea salt, or toasted pecans.

2	cups sugar, divided
½	cup cold butter, sliced
6	Tbsp. all-purpose flour
4	large egg yolks
2	cups milk
	Cream Cheese Pastry Shells
	Sweetened whipped cream

1. Cook 1 cup sugar in a medium-size heavy skillet over medium heat, stirring constantly, 6 to 8 minutes or until sugar melts and turns golden brown. Stir in butter until melted.

2. Whisk together flour, egg yolks, milk, and remaining 1 cup sugar in a 3-qt. heavy saucepan; bring just to a simmer over low heat, whisking constantly. Add sugar mixture to flour mixture, and cook, whisking constantly, 1 to 2 minutes or until thickened. Cover and chill 4 hours.

3. Meanwhile, prepare Cream Cheese Pastry Shells. Spoon caramel mixture into pastry shells, and top with whipped cream.

CREAM CHEESE PASTRY SHELLS

MAKES 6 DOZEN • HANDS-ON 35 MIN. • TOTAL 2 HR.

1	cup butter, softened
1	(8-oz.) package cream cheese, softened
3½	cups all-purpose flour

1. Beat butter and cream cheese at medium speed with a heavy-duty electric stand mixer until creamy. Gradually add flour to butter mixture, beating at low speed just until blended. Shape dough into 72 (¾-inch) balls, and place on a baking sheet; cover and chill 1 hour.

2. Preheat oven to 400°. Place dough balls in cups of lightly greased miniature muffin pans; press dough to top of cups, forming shells.

3. Bake at 400° for 10 to 12 minutes. Remove from pans to wire racks, and cool completely (about 15 minutes).

Tip: Baked pastry shells may be made up to one month ahead and frozen in an airtight container. Thaw at room temperature before filling.

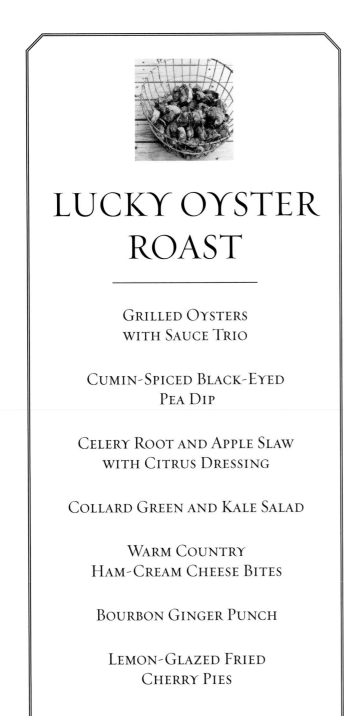

LUCKY OYSTER ROAST

GRILLED OYSTERS
WITH SAUCE TRIO

CUMIN-SPICED BLACK-EYED
PEA DIP

CELERY ROOT AND APPLE SLAW
WITH CITRUS DRESSING

COLLARD GREEN AND KALE SALAD

WARM COUNTRY
HAM-CREAM CHEESE BITES

BOURBON GINGER PUNCH

LEMON-GLAZED FRIED
CHERRY PIES

GRILLED OYSTERS WITH SAUCE TRIO

MAKES 10 SERVINGS • HANDS-ON 15 MIN. • TOTAL 2 HR., 5 MIN., INCLUDING SAUCES

10 dozen oysters
Pink Peppercorn Mignonette
Chimichurri Sauce
Roasted Tomato Chipotle Sauce

1. Preheat grill to 400° to 500° (high) heat.

2. Scrub oysters under running water; discard any that are open and do not close within seconds.

3. Grill oysters, covered with grill lid, about 5 minutes or until shells open slightly.

4. Pry off top shell, using oven mitts to protect hands from hot shells and liquid. Discard top shell, and loosen meat from bottom shell.

5. Place on a serving tray, and serve immediately with Pink Peppercorn Mignonette, Chimichurri Sauce, and Roasted Tomato Chipotle Sauce.

PINK PEPPERCORN MIGNONETTE

MAKES 1¼ CUPS · HANDS-ON 5 MIN. · TOTAL 35 MIN.

1   large shallot, minced

1½   Tbsp. crushed pink peppercorns

1   cup white wine vinegar

¼   tsp. kosher salt

1. Stir together shallot and next 3 ingredients in a small bowl. Let stand 30 minutes before serving.

CHIMICHURRI SAUCE

MAKES ABOUT 1⅓ CUPS · HANDS-ON 10 MIN. · TOTAL 10 MIN.

4   cups firmly packed fresh flat-leaf parsley leaves (about 1½ bunches)

¾   cup olive oil

4   garlic cloves

½   tsp. lime zest

¼   cup fresh lime juice

1   small shallot, chopped

1   tsp. kosher salt

½   tsp. dried crushed red pepper

½   tsp. freshly ground black pepper

1. Process all ingredients in a food processor until smooth. Let stand 30 minutes before serving.

ROASTED TOMATO CHIPOTLE SAUCE

MAKES ABOUT 1½ CUPS · HANDS-ON 15 MIN. · TOTAL 1 HR., 5 MIN.

8   plum tomatoes, cut into ½-inch-thick slices (about 2 lb.)

2   garlic cloves

2   Tbsp. olive oil, divided

½   tsp. kosher salt

¼   tsp. freshly ground black pepper

¼   cup loosely packed cilantro leaves

1   tsp. chopped chipotle pepper in adobo sauce

2   tsp. adobo sauce

1. Preheat oven to 300°. Arrange tomato slices in a single layer on a lightly greased large rimmed baking sheet; top with garlic cloves, and drizzle with 1 Tbsp. olive oil. Sprinkle salt and pepper evenly over top.

2. Bake at 300° for 50 to 60 minutes or until edges are lightly browned. Let cool slightly. Transfer mixture to a food processor. Add remaining 1 Tbsp. olive oil, cilantro, chipotle pepper, and adobo sauce; process until smooth. Season to taste with salt and pepper. Cover and refrigerate up to 2 days, if desired.

CUMIN-SPICED BLACK-EYED PEA DIP

MAKES 3¼ CUPS · HANDS-ON 15 MIN. · TOTAL 15 MIN.

2   garlic cloves

½   cup fresh lemon juice (about 2 lemons)

⅓   cup tahini paste

1   tsp. table salt

½   tsp. ground cumin

½   tsp. smoked paprika

2   (15.5-oz.) cans black-eyed peas, drained and rinsed

2   Tbsp. chopped fresh mint

2   Tbsp. extra virgin olive oil

Assorted crackers, radishes, carrots, celery

1. Process garlic, ¼ cup water, lemon juice, and next 6 ingredients in a food processor until smooth. Cover and chill up to 2 days.

2. Drizzle with extra virgin olive oil before serving with crackers, radishes, carrots, and celery.

Celery Root and Apple Slaw with Citrus Dressing

MAKES 10 TO 12 SERVINGS · HANDS-ON 20 MIN. · TOTAL 35 MIN.

1 tsp. orange zest

1/3 cup fresh orange juice

1/4 cup mayonnaise

2 Tbsp. olive oil

2 tsp. Creole mustard

1/8 tsp. paprika

1/2 tsp. table salt

1/2 tsp. freshly ground black pepper

1 lb. celery root, peeled

2 Gala apples, cut into matchstick-sized pieces

3 green onions, chopped

1. Whisk together orange zest and next 7 ingredients in a large bowl.

2. Shred celery root on large side of box grater. Toss with dressing, and stir in apples and green onions. Let stand 15 minutes before serving, or cover and refrigerate overnight.

Collard Green and Kale Salad

MAKES 10 TO 12 SERVINGS · HANDS-ON 30 MIN. · TOTAL 1 HR.

The heartiness of the greens in this salad makes it perfect for casual entertaining—the winter greens won't wilt as quickly as a summer greens salad.

1½ lb. sweet potatoes

1½ Tbsp. olive oil

1/2 tsp. kosher salt

1/4 tsp. freshly ground black pepper

1 Tbsp. butter

1 red onion, thinly sliced

2 Tbsp. brown sugar

1 Tbsp. apple cider vinegar

1 cup redskin natural raw peanuts

1/2 cup sugar

Wax paper

1 (5-oz.) package baby kale salad greens

3 cups thinly sliced fresh collard greens

1/2 cup sweetened dried cranberries

1 (4-oz.) package goat cheese, crumbled

Sorghum-Cider Vinaigrette

1. Preheat oven to 400°. Peel sweet potatoes, and cut into 1-inch cubes. Toss sweet potatoes with olive oil, salt, and pepper. Place on a lightly greased rimmed baking sheet.

2. Bake at 400°, stirring occasionally, for 35 to 40 minutes or until tender and lightly browned. Let cool to room temperature.

3. Melt butter in a medium skillet over medium heat; add onion slices. Cook 10 minutes, stirring occasionally. Add brown sugar, and cook 2 minutes. Add vinegar, stirring frequently, and cook 2 more minutes or until liquid is thickened. Remove from heat, and let cool.

4. Stir together peanuts and sugar in a medium skillet. Cook over medium heat 6 to 8 minutes, stirring often, until sugar is melted and peanuts are toasted. Transfer to a lightly greased wax paper-lined baking sheet. Let cool completely, and break into pieces.

5. Place kale and collard greens on a serving platter. Top with sweet potatoes, onions, peanuts, dried cranberries, goat cheese, and desired amount of Sorghum-Cider Vinaigrette.

Sorghum-Cider Vinaigrette

MAKES 1⅓ CUPS • HANDS-ON 10 MIN. • TOTAL 10 MIN.

¼ cup sorghum syrup

⅓ cup apple cider vinegar

½ tsp. kosher salt

½ tsp. freshly ground black pepper

¼ tsp. Worcestershire sauce

¾ cup olive oil

1. Whisk together sorghum syrup and next 4 ingredients in a medium bowl. Add oil in a slow, steady stream, whisking until smooth.

Warm Country Ham-Cream Cheese Bites

MAKES 45 TARTLETS • HANDS-ON 35 MIN. • TOTAL 53 MIN.

6 oz. shiitake mushrooms, stems removed and thinly sliced

⅔ cup diced country ham (about 2 oz.)

1 Tbsp. butter

1 (8-oz.) package cream cheese, softened

1 green onion, thinly sliced

3 (2.1-oz.) packages frozen mini phyllo pastry shells, thawed

1. Preheat oven to 350°. Sauté mushrooms and ham in butter in a medium skillet 8 minutes or until mushrooms are tender. Let cool 10 minutes.

2. Beat together cream cheese, mushroom mixture, and green onion at medium speed with an electric mixer until blended.

3. Place tarts on a large rimmed baking sheet. Fill each tart with about 2 tsp. cream cheese mixture.

4. Bake at 350° for 8 minutes or until cheese is melted.

Bourbon Ginger Punch

MAKES 8½ CUPS • HANDS-ON 15 MIN. • TOTAL 15 MIN.

½ cup sugar

1 cup fresh lime juice (about 4 limes)

2½ cups bourbon

3 (12-oz.) bottles ginger beer

Garnishes: lime wedges, maraschino cherries

1. Stir together ½ cup sugar and ½ cup water in a small saucepan. Cook over medium heat 5 minutes or just until sugar dissolves, stirring frequently. Let cool completely.

2. In a large pitcher, stir together simple syrup, lime juice, and bourbon; add ginger beer. Serve over ice.

LEMON-GLAZED FRIED CHERRY PIES

MAKES 10 PIES · HANDS-ON 45 MIN. · TOTAL 2 HR., 45 MIN.

5   cups all-purpose flour

1/3   cup sugar

1   Tbsp. baking powder

1/4   tsp. table salt

1/2   cup shortening, chilled and cut into pieces

1/4   cup butter, chilled and cut into pieces

1 1/3   cups cold water

2   (14-oz.) cans dark, sweet pitted cherries in heavy syrup, drained and chopped

1/3   cup cherry preserves

        Vegetable oil

2 1/2   cups powdered sugar

1   tsp. lemon zest

3   to 4 Tbsp. lemon juice

1/2   tsp. vanilla extract

1. Combine first 6 ingredients in a bowl with a pastry blender until crumbly. Sprinkle cold water, 1 Tbsp. at a time, over surface of mixture in bowl; stir with a fork until dry ingredients are moistened. Shape into a ball. Divide dough in half. Flatten each into a disk. Cover and chill 2 hours.

2. Stir together cherries and preserves.

3. Divide each disk into 5 pieces. Roll each piece on a lightly floured surface into a 6-inch circle.

4. Spoon about 3 tablespoons cherry mixture in center of each circle. Moisten outer 1/2-inch of circle with water. Fold round in half; press edges to seal, and crimp edges with a fork.

5. Pour oil to depth of 3 inches in a large Dutch oven. Heat to 350°. Fry pies, in batches, 2 minutes on each side or until golden. Place on a wire rack to drain.

6. Whisk together powdered sugar, lemon zest, juice, vanilla, and 1 Tbsp. water. Brush over warm pies immediately after frying. Let pies cool on wire rack.

Bourbon Ginger Punch

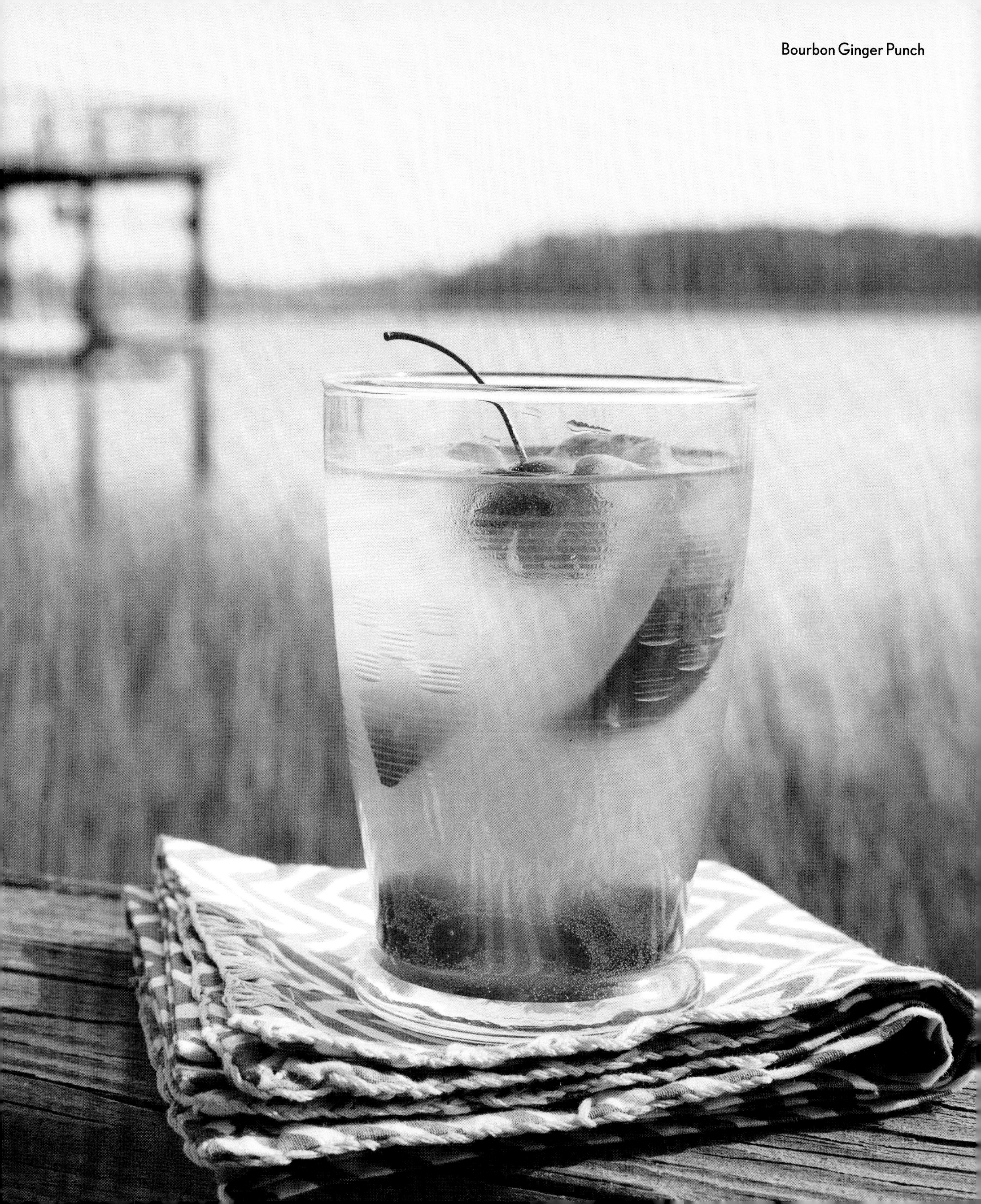

SANTA SIGHTING

Yes, Virginia, they do exist. Gathered for a photo at a recent convention are members of The Amalgamated Order of Real Bearded Santas, headquartered in Georgetown, Kentucky. Pictured from left: Santa, Santa, Santa, Santa, and Santa.

RECIPE INDEX

SUBJECT INDEX

W

TANNER LATHAM was born into a family of storytellers and grew up in a small town in northeast Alabama nestled in the foothills of the Appalachian Mountains. Stories, of course, were sacred—best shared at supper tables or on screened porches.

As travel editor for *Southern Living*, he wrote about distinctly Southern destinations, from cinder-block barbecue joints to luxurious five-star resorts. He has also worked as a reporter for NPR in Charlotte, North Carolina, producing on-air stories, slideshows, and multimedia videos. In his spare time, he hosts "Authentic South," (AuthenticSouth.com) a storytelling podcast that explores Southern culture through food, art, travel, music, and the fascinating characters who define the region.

KIM CROSS is an editor-at-large for *Southern Living* and a feature writer who has received awards from the Society of Professional Journalists, the Society of American Travel Writers, and the Media Industry Newsletter. Her writing has appeared in *Outside, Cooking Light, Bicycling, Runner's World, The Tampa Bay Times, The Birmingham News, The Anniston Star, USA TODAY, The New Orleans Times-Picayune,* and CNN.com. Her first book, *What Stands in a Storm,* is a literary nonfiction account of the biggest tornado outbreak in the history of recorded weather.

RICK BRAGG is the author of three critically acclaimed and best-selling books, *All Over but the Shoutin', Ava's Man,* and *The Prince of Frogtown.* His most recent book, *The Most They Ever Had,* is an eloquent tale of an Alabama cotton mill community. A native Alabamian, Bragg says he learned to tell stories by listening to the masters, the people of the foothills of the Appalachians.

During his career, Bragg worked at several newspapers before joining *The New York Times* in 1994. In 1992, he was awarded a Nieman Fellowship at Harvard University. As a national correspondent for the *Times,* Bragg won the 1996 Pulitzer Prize for Feature Writing. In addition, he has twice won the prestigious American Society of Newspaper Editors Distinguished Writing Award, along with more than 50 other writing awards.

Currently, Bragg is a Professor of Writing in the Journalism Department at the University of Alabama, where he teaches Advanced Magazine Writing and Narrative Nonfiction.

ACKNOWLEDGMENTS

We'd like to extend our gratitude to the individuals who contributed their time and talents to help create this book.

Special thanks to the book's dedicated photo team for their beautiful work and cooperative spirit:
Iain Bagwell, Photographer; Lydia DeGaris Pursell, Stylist; and Ana Price Kelly, Food Stylist.

PHOTOGRAPHERS

Lucas Allen
Ralph Anderson
Iain Bagwell
Jim Bathie
Beall + Thomas Photography
Monica Buck
Robbie Caponetto
Van Chaplin
Gary Clark
Crown Center/William
  & Jill DiMartino
Jennifer Davick
Erica George Dines
Peter Frank Edwards
Roger Foley
Jim Franco
Laurey W. Glenn
David Greear
Courtesy of The Greenbrier
Rush Jagoe
Kansas City Convention
  and Visitors Association
Klaas Lingbeek-van Kranen/Getty
  Images
Becky Luigart-Stayner
Art Meripol
Meg McKinney
Helen Norman
Courtesy of The Omni Homestead
  Resort
Chris Rogers

Hector Sanchez
Mark Sandlin
Steffen Schnur/Getty Images
Mary Britton Senseney
Christopher Shane
Scott Suchman
Jason Wallis
Diana Zalucky
Cheryl Zibiski

FOOD STYLISTS

Marian Cooper Cairns
Ashley Strickland Freeman
Ana Price Kelly
Vanessa McNeil Rocchio
Maggie Ruggiero
Angela Sellers

PHOTO STYLISTS

Stacy Allen
Lindsey Ellis Beatty
Jennifer Berno
Amy Burke
Kay E. Clarke
Caroline M. Cunningham
Elizabeth Demos
Marie-Laure Coste Dujols
Matthew Gleason
Libba Hardwick
Jimmie Henslee

Heather Chadduck Hillegas
Phoebe Howard
Sissy Lamberton
Buffy Hargett Miller
Dickie Morris
Lydia DeGaris Pursell
Rebecca Bull Reed
Pat Roberts
Sherry Spencer
Sybil Sylvester
Kimberly Schlegel Whitman

WRITERS

Paula Disbrowe
Sandy Lang

HOMEOWNERS

Calder and Chauncey Clark
Alice and Hamlet Fort
Genia and Glenn Gilchrist
Marianne and Steve Harrison
Seleta Hayes Howard and
  Peter Howard
Cindy and Don Waters

*Grateful appreciation to
Bromberg's, Birmingham, Alabama,
for their generosity and assistance
with photography for this book.

ISBN-13: 978-0-8487-4316-1
ISBN-10: 0-8487-4316-4
Library of Congress Control Number: 2014940462

Printed in the United States of America
First Printing 2014

OXMOOR HOUSE

Editorial Director: Leah McLaughlin
Creative Director: Felicity Keane
Art Director: Christopher Rhoads
Executive Food Director: Grace Parisi
Senior Editor: Rebecca Brennan
Managing Editor: Elizabeth Tyler Austin
Assistant Managing Editor: Jeanne de Lathouder

SOUTHERN LIVING®
CHRISTMAS ALL THROUGH THE SOUTH

Food Editor: Allison E. Cox
Project Editor: Lacie Pinyan
Assistant Test Kitchen Manager: Alyson Moreland Haynes
Recipe Developers and Testers: Tamara Goldis, Stefanie Maloney, Callie Nash, Karen Rankin, Leah Van Deren
Food Stylists: Victoria E. Cox, Margaret Monroe Dickey, Catherine Crowell Steele
Photography Director: Jim Bathie
Senior Photographer: Hélène Dujardin
Senior Photo Stylists: Kay E. Clarke, Mindi Shapiro Levine
Senior Production Manager: Sue Chodakiewicz
Production Manager: Theresa Beste-Farley

CONTRIBUTORS

Writers: Kim Cross, Tanner Latham
Brand Manager: Daniel Fagan
Junior Designer: Frances Higginbotham
Editorial Assistant: April Smitherman
Copy Editors: Donna Baldone, Julie H. Bosché
Calligraphers: Mary Elizabeth Davis, Katherine Ross
Indexer: Mary Ann Laurens
Recipe Developer and Tester: Lyda Burnette
Food Stylists: Ashley Strickland Freeman, Ana Price Kelly
Photographers: Iain Bagwell, Rush Jagoe, Art Meripol, Chris Rogers, Mary Britton Senseney, Christopher Shane, Scott Suchman, Jason Wallis
Photo Stylists: Elizabeth Demos, Lydia DeGaris Pursell
Photo Editors: Kellie Lindsey, Karen Williams
Fellows: Ali Carruba, Kylie Dazzo, Elizabeth Laseter, Anna Ramia, Deanna Sakal, Tonya West, Amanda Widis

SOUTHERN LIVING®

Editor: Sid Evans
Creative Director: Robert Perino
Managing Editor: Candace Higginbotham
Executive Editors: Hunter Lewis, Jessica S. Thuston
Deputy Food Director: Whitney Wright
Test Kitchen Director: Robby Melvin
Test Kitchen Specialist/Food Styling: Vanessa McNeil Rocchio
Test Kitchen Professional: Pam Lolley
Recipe Editor: JoAnn Weatherly
Style Director: Heather Chadduck Hillegas
Director of Photography: Jeanne Dozier Clayton
Photographers: Robbie Caponetto, Laurey W. Glenn, Hector Sanchez
Assistant Photo Editor: Kate Phillips Robertson
Photo Coordinator: Chris Ellenbogen
Senior Photo Stylist: Buffy Hargett Miller
Assistant Photo Stylist: Caroline Murphey Cunningham
Photo Administrative Assistant: Courtney Authement
Editorial Assistant: Pat York

TIME HOME ENTERTAINMENT INC.

President and Publisher: Jim Childs
Vice President and Associate Publisher: Margot Schupf
Vice President, Finance: Vandana Patel
Executive Director, Marketing Services: Carol Pittard
Publishing Director: Megan Pearlman
Assistant General Counsel: Simone Procas